PLACES

An Anthology of Britain

JAMES H. CHAMBERS
6323 MARY JAMISON DR
SAN ANTONIO, TX. 78238

PLACES

An Anthology of Britain

CHOSEN BY RONALD BLYTHE

Oxford New York Toronto Melbourne

OXFORD UNIVERSITY PRESS

1981

Oxford University Press, Walton Street, Oxford OX2 6DP

London Glasgow New York Toronto
Delhi Bombay Calcutta Madras Karachi
Kuala Lumpur Singapore Hong Kong Tokyo
Nairobi Dar es Salaam Cape Town
Melbourne Wellington
and associate companies in
Beirut Berlin Ibadan Mexico City

Pieces previously published elsewhere:
Padstow by Sir John Betjeman from First and Last Loves
(John Murray, 1952)
Here by Philip Larkin from The Whitsun Weddings
(Faber & Faber, 1964)
Barchester Lives On by Jan Morris,
an article in The Times

British Library Cataloguing in Publication Data
Places.
1. English poetry—20th century
2. Great Britain—Poetry
3. English essays—20th century
I. Blythe, Ronald
821'.9'1208032   PR1195.G/   80-49735
ISBN 0-19-211575-8

Title-page illustration: Holkham Hall, Norfolk by John Piper

Set by Western Printing Services Ltd
Printed in Great Britain
at the University Press, Oxford
by Eric Buckley
Printer to the University

For Jane and Denis Garrett

FOREWORD

This anthology is a present to Oxfam from its many distinguished contributors, poets, novelists, historians, photographers, and the artist John Piper, all of whom gave their work free in order that its profits can go to a charity whose long and loving usefulness in a wicked world goes from strength to strength. Except for familiar inclusions such as Philip Larkin's *Here*, John Betjeman's *Padstow*, and Jan Morris's *Barchester Lives On*, chosen by the editor simply because they are favourites of his (anthologists are very self-indulgent), and whose royalties in this instance have been generously made over to Oxfam, all the essays and poems were written for or first published in this collection. Their common theme is that of personal geography, both urban and rural. Whenever we manage to place ourselves, imaginatively speaking, into the situations of individuals who make up those pitiful armies of war- and storm-scattered humanity which Oxfam has fed and clothed during the past almost forty years, it is natural that we should view their plight in terms chiefly of hunger and shelter. But what of being forced out of one's own landscape? This has been the fate of millions in our own day, and for many it has been the worst disaster of all. So an eloquent appreciation and defence of place in its most personal terms makes a very proper theme for a book such as this.

It was the Deputy Director of Oxfam, Guy Stringer, together with Richard Stanley, who originally conceived the idea, and it has been my very real pleasure to make it tangible. The response by the many distinguished writers and photographers invited to participate in such a venture exceeded anything I could have hoped would have happened when I took the task on, and I am enormously indebted to them for joining me in a project which attempts to give Oxfam a kind of literary 'thank you' for all that it has achieved since the 1940s. I cannot praise them enough for first so entirely understanding what was required—and then providing it.

The first contribution to arrive was from R. S. Thomas and almost the last from Barbara Pym, splendid novelist and now sadly no more. The extract from her Diary and the witty letters which accompanied it gave no indication that her kind participation in this anthology would be her final work. In between there arrived a remarkable variety of place-poetry and place-prose from writers I have long admired, and when John Piper said he would give me some beautiful paintings and the jacket, I felt that no anthologist could want for more. The generosity of everyone concerned with *Places* has been an impressive experience for me and I am most grateful.

Because it could be an example of something being so familiar that it can no longer be seen, I should add a reminding word or two about Oxfam. Although it now operates on a heroic scale it has been able to retain an intimate and even a parochial quality. It is both highly professional in its operations—consider its activities during the Seventies which spanned the Bangladesh disaster and the man-made horror of Cambodia—and also approachably amateur, so that practically anyone of good will still finds it quite an ordinary and natural business to give it a helping hand. It has come a long way since the day in 1942 when Gilbert Murray and his colleagues, anxious about Greek refugees, met in the Quaker meeting-house at Oxford to organize food and clothes, calling themselves The Oxford Committee for Famine Relief. Almost at once the British government stopped their aid because, it said, some of it would be sure to benefit the enemy. Ever since, the organization has needed to fight running battles with politicians of all kinds, and in all lands, in its insistence that its stance is apolitical where basic human wants are concerned. Thus began its long commitment: to the Palestinian refugees of 1949, the Koreans in 1950, the British East Coast floods of 1953, the Hungarian refugees of 1956; its significant role during World Refugee Year in 1959, in the Congo in 1960, Biafra in 1967–70, the 'hidden famine' in Ethiopia during 1973, the Guatemalan earthquake of 1976, the Indian cyclone of 1977, and hundreds of other upheavals of all kinds, as well as involvement in the great shifts and changes in international welfare and education generally. It is among the finest records of human brotherliness. This literary evocation of some of our own landscape has been gathered together both to add something to Oxfam's ceaselessly called-upon fund and as a tribute.

R.B.

CONTENTS

Contents

ILLUSTRATIONS

BY JOHN PIPER

PHOTOGRAPHS

SIX HOUSES

Ay, now am I in Arden; the more fool I:
when I was at home, I was in a better place:
but travellers must be content.

As You Like It, II. iv. 16.

Stonor Park, Oxfordshire by John Piper

Our Hainault Forest

RUTH PITTER

'But Hainault is one of the proudest names in Europe!' exclaimed C. S. Lewis when he heard it. Yes: a queen (Philippa, consort of Edward III) who bore that proud name did actually own a 'bower' (country house) at Havering, whose full name is Havering-atte-Bower. Havering would have been well within the Forest then, though now it is a howling suburb.

By the time we first knew Hainault Forest (in the first decade of this century) it had dwindled to a square mile or two of actual woodland, plus about an equal area of open grassland that had been forest, and was beginning to be replanted. The actual woodland, and I believe it is primeval forest, consists of hornbeam, invariably pollard, some oak and holly, here and there a crabtree. (No beech, unlike Epping.) William Morris was strong on hornbeam. I believe he said there wasn't much of it anywhere, let alone hornbeam forest.

Until we moved away from Goodmayes (about three miles south) Hainault was our Eden. Before the motor car, and indeed mostly afterwards, we had to walk, either the direct way or partly by train, when we were glad to sit down under the first big oak to eat lunch, and not get very much further.

That was when we were children. As we explored further we discovered Crabtree Hill, where there were three cottages—*and one of them was empty*. Frantically we besought our parents to find out who owned it, and to rent it if possible. Passionately we children affirmed that we should never want another seaside holiday, if we could only have that cottage. We never did.

There was no road to it—no main road, though the rooty track was officially regarded as such. One approached downhill, through the trees, across a brook, then up a steep grass slope. The poor old place would seem very forlorn as we entered, but a fire once lit, beds warmed, and a meal organized, it was a home indeed: all the better, somehow, for being minimal. A hole that only just fits is safer.

In addition to weekends, we would spend the whole of the summer holidays up there, our poor parents commuting during the last week or two, when their primary schools started before our secondary ones. I like to remember how earnestly we three made sure that everything was ready for a substantial tea before these heroic parents (who had started at dawn, foot-slogged the three miles to the station, taught some of the poorest of London children all day among the stinking factories of Old Ford, returned by slow train, and foot-slogged the three miles again) could be expected to appear. We would hear our father's queer cry (a sort of whoop, he couldn't whistle) from the bosky wood, and instantly make the tea, as the dears would then arrive just as this was properly infused.

There was a day during one of these end-of-holiday periods that I have never forgotten, it was so perfect in its way. After our parents had left, we three (two girls and a boy) set off to walk to Romford market. Through the forest, over the fields, then a farm track, a lane, and at last a road, with all kinds of horse-drawn vehicles, pigs in carts, and poor cattle being driven. A lovely autumn day, with the hedges full of berries and wild flowers. We spent most of the day in the town, gloated over the stalls where men were making huge slabs of toffee, averted our eyes from the poor livestock, and rejoiced to see the farmers, and drovers, and gypsies in all their rich variety. We ate our sandwiches sitting on some nice quiet tombstones, and then it was time to buy some of the famous sausages and cakes, and to think of turning homeward. (We always thought of the cottage as *home*, of the suburban house as a *pied-à-terre*.) It was getting duskish when we crossed the stile into the forest, and darkish by the time we reached the cottage. But our timing was good—father's whoop was heard, and the gleam of his lantern seen, just as the kettle boiled, the sausages were exactly right, the toast in perfection. A jewel of a day!

The 1914 War came, and we were gladder than ever of our quiet little refuge, though our mother didn't feel safe from the Zepps anywhere—until we saw the first one brought down (by Lieutenant Leefe Robinson, flying the crate of the period, and firing, it was said, common Guy Fawkes squibs from bits of gas-piping). We saw the lovely airship luminous in searchlights, and then—a bright spot on the envelope, a flame that ran swiftly, and an awful shapeless torch drifting down the sky, lighting up everything as bright as day—every leaf, every flower in the garden in brilliant colour. A minute's awful silence as the horrible light faded, and then, out of the dark, a great cheer from the gun crew in the Forest. They then sang the Doxology, which is more than they would do now. People set off to the scene, we were told, and brought back things. . . .

On public holidays, before the buses began running out into the surrounding villages, horse-drawn charabancs used to bring out loads of people, but they were no trouble; they never went out of sight of the pubs. I think they utterly lost their bearings once the trees had closed round them. But when the buses started, there would be quite a number of people throughout the Forest, and we would tend to retreat inside our defences. Often there would be enquiries for tea. We three would gladly have turned an honest penny in this way, but we were not allowed. Now the Forest on a warm day was very tiring and dehydrating, and something more; it could really exhaust and drain one, and in such a case there is nothing like tea, nothing at all.

On one occasion at least I seem to remember that we children made tea on the sly in the old outhouse, and sneaked it out—not to get money, we would take none—but because we had met among the trees a couple who moved our tough hearts strangely. They were not very young, but they were rather beautiful, and their clothes had something of a story-book effect. They asked charmingly about possible tea. We could tell that the lady at least really needed tea—after all, we had a mother—and we dimly sensed that the gentleman was inwardly praying for her sake that we would provide it. I am so glad that we broke the rules for them. Those lovers, if they had lived so long, would be over a hundred years old now. Peace be to them.

They belonged to the Forest, for after all it was the romantics, the poetic people, who liked to get well into the woodland:

> . . . fade away into the forest dim.
> Fade far away, dissolve, and quite forget . . .
> Keats, *Ode to a Nightingale*

For such people it was worthwhile to come in the winter, for then the dear Forest closed round one like kind arms, with its warmth and shelter and solitude, and the exhausting atmosphere of summer was forgotten. On a bright February day it could be lovely on the south side of the thickets, sitting in the dry bracken to eat lunch, but just round the corner—ugh!

7

We bade farewell to the dear old place when our widowed mother retired from teaching and wished to move into mid-Essex. Years afterwards, on the point of leaving London and its environs for ever, I organized a farewell picnic, and for once I *did* organize. On an idyllic September day, my sister and I, with a couple of friends, took train to Ilford, sprinted for a bus, rode to Cabin Plain, walked to a nice hut made of furze-faggots, had a splendid lunch (with a libation), went through the woodland (now sprinkled with bomb-holes) to look at the cottage, now of course in other hands; then over the fields to the ancient little church, where we finished our provisions under the cedar near our father's grave; then fields again, now blessedly downhill, into Abridge, where we caught a bus that took us well into London. I had planned it right; the weather had been perfect, and it all worked like a charm. There was no grief in the farewell, for we had been so permanently enriched by the Forest, that we carry it in us until the end of our pilgrimage.

Somewhere

GEORGE MACBETH

In all those rooms, no light
Unfiltered by the trees.
Only the broken spears
Of sunlight through smudged glass:
And windows dimmed with webs.

Across the road, thin sheep
And a church behind its yews.
Weeds to a crumbled wall
And an undergrowth of grass
Great roots of beech lay bare.

Somewhere

Indoors, the musty smell
Of old wood drying through
And forgotten food left out.
Sour milk in open cups.
Dead bread along a board.

There are many beds unmade
In that exotic house.
The remains of passengers
Whose lives have fallen in
And thrown them out to the sky.

In the attics, time has knelt
And driven holes through jars.
The scum of paint in tins
Tells of a former care
That blistered in the halls.

A foot of green slime swills
In the cellar by the stairs.
Brick arches built for wine
Are in water to their knees
And toads now croak for port.

Here, on the barren floors,
The vapid slap of soles
Remainders gaiety
To the drone of testy flies.
Even the cat's foot slurs

In unfurnished corridors
And the hinges of the doors
Creak with a hidden weight.
There is black, unmanaged soot
On the ostrich of each grate.

Six Houses

Whoever used these rooms
Has abandoned them to the air.
Air, and the stink of rats.
But outside, the long gallery
Of chestnuts rustles leaves

And the garden gives away
What the mansion chose to lose,
A sense of grand repose.
The stately lines of pride
From a rectitude of prayer

Are simplified to the shape
Of a summer's afternoon
Where growth is an elegance
And people come to read
In the shadow of old trees.

Walking, and loving these,
In the gentle wind and the heat,
May be all that remains to aid
Or obliterate the decay.
It seems so, this summer's day.

Top Withers, near Haworth, West Yorkshire by Fay Godwin

The House in the Hythe

RICHARD COBB

I would like to express my warmest thanks to my sister, Mrs Diana Papé, for the help that she provided me in the preparation of this essay on the Hythe, Colchester, in the time of our grandparents. Seven years older than myself, she knew 'Charlie' and 'Mrs Ma' and St. Leonard's House from 1909 to 1928, nineteen years, whereas my recollection of them was limited to only eleven years. I hope that I have recorded her memories and impressions with accuracy and sympathy.

My grandparents, Charles and Catherine Cobb, managed to prolong the nineteenth century into the first twenty-eight years of the present one. Or it could be put the other way round: that they succeeded in excluding the twentieth century pretty well up to the year 1928. Certainly their daily timetable and general manner of life could be taken as a warning to historians not to attach too much importance to the beginning or the end of a century as a particularly significant dividing line in neatly cut-up periods. My grandparents were Victorians, and remained so under Edward VII and George V; indeed my grandfather was born in 1837, as if to emphasize the fact (my grandmother, one year older, dated back to William IV). So they were among the minority of people scarcely to have been affected by the First World War, an event of which they must, however, have been aware, as their eldest son, Primus, who had always lived at home, and had never done any work after spending one year as a ship's engineer as a young man, went to work at Paxman's munition factory (it was just beyond the garden), and my grandfather had had himself driven over in his gig to White Colne, to see the still smoking remains of a Zeppelin that had been shot down. Moreover he would have had to interrupt his biannual business trips to Brussels (via Parkeston and the Hook). Rumours of an impending German landing on the low-lying coast of Little Holland may even have penetrated as far inland as the Hythe, brought there by my mother from my birthplace at Frinton on Sea (where everyone kept a bag packed with night things and a change of clothing, in the event of a sudden evacuation; but, in Colchester, this precaution was not considered necessary). But such rumours would scarcely have ruffled the walled calm and regularity of St. Leonard's House and its garden, the daylight hours marked out by the gentle cooing of my grandmother's white Barbary doves, in their green dovecot at the near end of the garden. Already, by 1914, they were both so old as to be well beyond the extensive age group to find its names on rural or urban War Memorials; and it is likely that, good Victorians as they were, they regarded the great conflagration with the same disapproval, as an example of juvenile savagery and folly, as they had previously shown for the foolish war in the Transvaal. I do not really know, as I never once heard them refer to the events of 1914–18.

In this eminently reassuring continuity, they were as much protected by their physical environment and by their numerous personal entourage: Primus, the eldest son, living in, himself a sort of superior house servant (he rang the gong, ordered the menus, and made rugs); Daisy Tawell, my grandfather's niece, taken in when her parents had been killed in a carriage accident, and who only moved from her room at the top of the house to attend meals, or to expose her faded good looks and neglected linen to the gaze of the Hythe when on her 'parish work', contained in a small basket; three house servants: Ellen, the daily, Louisa, the house parlourmaid, and Elizabeth, the cook; and Mills, the groom, who, according to rumour, had taken part in the Crimean War, as by their own engrossing mutual understanding and affection which enabled them to divide the house and its functions into two clearly delineated territories. The breakfast room, at the front, was strictly masculine, the drawing-room was my grandmother's social kingdom downstairs, the dining-room was shared, the stables went by right to my grandfather. It was the same with their weekly activities: the only one shared was attendance at matins and evensong on Sundays at St. Leonard's Church (the tower of which could be seen above the garden wall). Entertaining the 'Divines' to tea was my grandmother's province. And she had herself driven out by Mills, in the gig, and wearing a bonnet and veil and a black silk dress, on various charitable missions among the narrow alley-ways that lead off Hythe Hill. Her husband attended a club, went out shooting. Every September, he went to Scotland. Their lives were parallel, rather than shared, and, although they lived in the same house, for very many years, they lived in different parts of it.

St. Leonard's House was the largest in the Hythe, larger than the Rectory or the brick house occupied by the manager of the gasworks. But it was near the bottom of Hythe Hill, which, as it ran down towards the Colne and the harbour, descended likewise into want, dirt, poverty, and noisy drunkenness. The two bow-windows of the house faced across the street on to two adjacent pubs, equally crowded, and with men constantly going from the one to the other; seen through the dining-room window, which had little rounds of glass, the two pubs seemed to move, like jellies, while the figures coming and going became foreshortened, as if seen in comic mirrors at a fair. From the first floor, the bow-windows commanded a clear view up and down the Hill, almost as if one were in the path of the clattering green tram. On each side of the house were two-storeyed shops—Steggles's, the grocer's, and a chandler's, and artisans' cottages. The sheer size of the house and its ornate Georgian porch might have seemed a provocation to a neighbourhood probably the poorest in Colchester. But it was not so; the house aroused respect, not rancour.

It was a large, rambling, brick place, early Georgian, four or five storeys, though 'storey' would be an over-simplification for a house that had a whole series of different grades of level and the floors and ceilings of which curved in odd ways, putting the furniture at peculiar angles: three steps down here, six steps up there, tiny corridors that screwed around, dark doors opening on to equally dark, miniature staircases, as if the house itself was constantly trying to assert its privacy and was attempting to escape from itself. It was a permanent source of amazement to me that my grandparents, who were already in their late eighties when I first became aware of their benevolent care, did not break their legs or turn their ankles in such an ill-lit maze of traps, double-doors, and musty passages. There was even a Ghost Cupboard—in fact a room over the archway connecting the house with the stables, used to store broken furniture, old curtains and covers, and rejected china, the varied debris of very many years; because it perched over a void, and because the doors at each end were very seldom opened, the room was not so much frightening as mysterious; it was rather like a tiny room over a church porch, and so I greatly enjoyed sitting in it, looking out either on to the stable-yard or on to the street; and it was especially exciting to see the gig disappear underneath, as if I were on a bridge.

Even the day-nursery, which at one time had been my father's room (a fact recalled by the presence, under the window-seat, of his sword from the Boer War, covered in oil, and wrapped up in a cloth; and, in a green tin trunk, of his green-lined white topee and his long red underpants and red vests—I asked my mother about the colour, and she told me red kept out the heat, so I supposed that all our Empire-builders wore red underneath), was on three different levels, rising to a sort of stage that commanded the bow-window, with its view on to the two pubs and the Hill. It reminded me of what I thought must have been the view from the captain's quarters in an eighteenth-century man-of-war. The bathroom, at the top of the house, overlooking the garden, was entered by three steps downwards. The main staircase and the many minor ones all played different tunes, the floorboards in my bedroom creaked with a full range of sounds; and on the wall of the main staircase there was a long, squiggly black line, like the sluggish course of the Colne, and that had been plastered over, a split that ran from top to bottom and that dated from the great Essex Earthquake of 1884.

My grandparents spent most of their indoor lives in the half of the house that faced inwards, away from the street and onto the long walled garden. Their bedrooms and their dressing-rooms, cut off from the rest of the house by two green-baize doors, as if to insulate them from the noise of Hythe Hill, were *côté-jardin*, at night a pool of silence. So was my grandmother's drawing-room, on the ground floor. Primus too had a bedroom and a dressing-room in some mysterious corner on the garden side, in an *entresol* between the third and fourth storeys. Daisy was right at the top, in a bedroom as impenetrable as the others on the silent side, though my sister once managed to get into it, when its occupant was out, after having shot an arrow through its (rarely) open window. (Daisy was none too clean, and liked a fug.)

My grandparents, Primus, and Daisy only moved over to the street side for meals, though even these were not all held together and in the same place. At eight, my grandparents, Tim-Tom, my grandmother's cat, and, when we were staying there, my mother, sister, and I, had breakfast in the dining-room: bacon, kidneys, sausages, partridge pie (when in season) were laid out on the

15

sideboard for the grown-ups to help themselves, having first had porridge; and there was a silver methylated egg-boiler on the table, with egg cups and spoons all round. We sat at our places, and the cat walked all over the table, given tit-bits by our grandmother. At nine, Primus had breakfast by himself in the breakfast room, a small, dark, leathery, very masculine room on the opposite side of the corridor, and sunken below street level, giving a rather murky view on to the feet, shins, and the middles of passers-by who, from inside, appeared to be headless. His lonely, but copious, meal was witnessed by a large print depicting the Tranby Croft Scandal: Tranby Croft observed my uncle, I don't think he ever observed Tranby Croft, his head well down in the steady and regularly timed absorption of a breakfast that progressed from porridge, kipper, sausage, kidney, egg and bacon, to toast and marmalade. At ten, Daisy, her hair in curlers (she only took them off on her thrice-weekly excursions out of doors on 'parish business') had her breakfast alone in the dining-room. But lunch and dinner were family meals, 'gonged' by Primus, after checking his watch with the grandfather clock, and both with the clock on the tower of St. Leonard's. My grandmother had tea in her drawing-room; my sister and I were often admitted to this very elaborate ceremony, after which we would be read to (I heard there the whole of *Little Dorrit*, in every-other-day instalments, and producing, on my part, every-other-day tears). But first there would be a close inspection of our nails, faces, and clothing. Having to go to bed early (and alone, in a huge four-poster, surrounded by heavy curtains), I never discovered where my grandparents, Primus, and Daisy spent their evenings, after supper, and before going to bed (which Primus did at nine-thirty). I *think* my grandfather and his eldest son retired to the breakfast room, as it was also called the smoke room (and it certainly smelt of smoke and cigars, as well as of kipper and leather, in the morning). My grandmother presumably went off to her drawing-room; and Daisy went up to bed (where she also spent much of the day, fully clothed, smoking, and catching up on Teddy Tail of the *Daily Mail*, her only reading, apart from the Book of Common Prayer; Primus's only reading were the obituaries in the *Essex County Standard*). But, so my sister tells me—and seven years my senior, she was an earlier witness—Daisy sometimes accompanied herself on the piano in my grandmother's drawing-room.

16

The House in the Hythe

Here then were four people, firmly fixed in their ways, their territories, their timetables, their *sorties* (in the case of my grandmother, as elaborate as rare), their activities (or, in the case of Daisy, the lack of them), long before either my sister or I came on the scene. It must have been gradually worked out, almost by touch, back in the 1890s or the 1900s, though I daresay conventions had hardened and become increasingly frozen with time. There *had* been gradual changes: according to my mother, rather a hostile witness, Daisy spent more and more time in bed and became more and more neglectful of soap. Primus had certainly become odder, more withdrawn, more taciturn, and more obsessed with checking up on the exact time, while his rug-making increased, his products gradually filling the house. At some previous stage, his father had ceased to address him directly, communicating only in the third person: 'Primus will wind up the clock' (not that Primus needed any telling), 'Primus will call for the library books', 'Primus will consult the glass'. Primus would address his mother as 'Mrs Ma', who, in return, called him 'Herbert dear', or 'dear Primus'; but Primus never addressed his father, and my grandmother never addressed Daisy. But my grandfather never failed to greet his niece, with a quite genuine warmth—she was his ward—when she emerged downstairs at ten, even asking her what she was going to do, though this must have been something of a formality, for he did not wait for the answer, which would generally have been 'nothing'. My mother, when present, would try to talk to everybody, thereby breaking a number of long-recognized House Rules, and causing my father—in any case very rarely present—a certain embarrassment. My mother proclaimed the need 'to draw Primus out', but out he would not be drawn, even under her direct questioning, *with*drawing silently, with his bobbins, needles and stuff, to the breakfast room or to his fortress somewhere upstairs on the garden side (I think he too qualified for a green-baize door). Primus and my father and the middle brother, Arthur (a rare visitor, who worked in Southwold), had whispered conversations, in which there were oblique references to 'the Guv'nor', when they met on one of the many landings or dark staircases. But Primus and my father cannot have had much to say to each other, the latter having spent most of his life away from the Hythe, indeed from England, his eldest brother showing the greatest reluctance ever to absent himself from

17

the house for more than twenty minutes, the statutory time he assigned to his twice-daily walks or to shopping. The two walks never varied: morning through the footpath past Paxman's and the lime pit, turn by the blind donkey, to the duck pond, back the same way: afternoon, to the harbour, as far as the gasworks, back the same way.

My grandparents addressed one another as 'Charlie' and 'Mrs Ma'. They even had quite long conversations about Colchester affairs, my grandmother questioning 'Charlie' about his friends 'up town', a very distant territory which exercised some fascination for her, but which she had not visited for many years. But my grandfather would avoid any topic concerned with kitchen affairs; and Mills, the stables, and the mare Jenny, would remain beyond my grandmother's enquiries or criticisms. When 'the Guv'nor' announced—as he did once or twice a month, after one of the groom's regular drinking-bouts—that Mills had been sacked, the appalling sentence would be received in silence, as would that, the next day, that he had been reinstalled and 'given another chance'. Mills certainly had had a great many 'chances' since Crimean days. The garden, on the other hand, was a recognized common topic between them, though it was also—like the interior of the house—shared out territorially, the potted geraniums and the doves the domain of the old lady, the greenhouse and orchard and the men's lavatory by the wood-shed at the far end, that of the old gentleman (my sister was given strict instructions never to play in that end of the garden), the lawn and the shrubbery, common ground. Tim-Tom, the large, and very aged—nearly twenty when he died, as if in homage to his master and mistress—black cat, who had earlier survived falling through the glass roof of the scullery, in a sudden leap from the bathroom window, frightened by the sudden shriek of the geyser, an antique, shining, brass instrument, was an interest also shared between them (as was also an equally aged Labrador, born the same day as my sister), though Tim-Tom had a special chair in the old lady's drawing-room and was rumoured to sleep in the old man's dressing-room. Tim-Tom was perhaps the only inhabitant to have the whole house as his territory, ranging from drawing-room to the kitchen, from dressing-room to dressing-room, from the dining-room table to that of the breakfast room (he attended all three breakfasts, as well as lunch and supper,

18

on the table, participating in the meals, if not in the somewhat limited conversation). The 'Divines', Canon Carter, the Vicar of St. Leonard's, and the Revd Gilbert Newcummen, his companion, were the special conversational concern of the old lady. Although the old man was a regular churchgoer and a churchwarden, he did not seem quite at ease with the Revd Mr Newcummen, whom he may have regarded as effeminate. I certainly found his appearance very extraordinary, for he had a red wig, which was not always on straight, wore starched frills round his clerical collar, and had rows of little buttons down his front. It is possible that my grandfather felt social concern for the 'Divines' was the proper function of the lady of the house.

My sister and I were not subjected to any of these unstated House Rules, though the former, seven years older than myself, was not only aware of them, but took a malicious pleasure in breaching them. We were both allowed to prattle away at table, often to the visible amusement of our grandparents, though neither of us ever succeeded in breaking the sombre, stony taciturnity of Primus, or the cottony daydreams of Daisy, who would, however, find animation and even voice at the sight of gooseberry jam. She had a sweet tooth, like a child of ten or so, which, in many ways, is what she had remained. I think I was too overawed by the solemnity and ceremony of these family meals—with a full display of silver tureens, cruets, and some rather mysterious objects: a silver fish with a ring through its nose, a silver swan, its feathers fanning out—to profit much from such indulgence. My sister claims that, at six or seven, I was as taciturn as my uncle. But I can recall one occasion when, having come in very excited, and with the feeling of having something important to communicate, I not only spoke, but insisted on being heard by the old man, who was rather deaf. I had been out 'shopping'—or so it was called—with Mills in the gig. On the way back, coming down Clyngo Hill, Jenny had stumbled and fallen, nearly tipping us both out (I was strapped in next to Mills). I announced this, as an item of original news, in the middle of lunch: 'Gee-gee Jenny had a fall', repeating it till I was quite sure my grandfather had heard. I could see no harm in the statement, but the old man was very angry, and Mills was sacked on the spot (to be reinstated the same evening).

Before my time, when they had both been more active, my

19

grandparents had had quite a wide circle of friends. I have seen photographs of shooting parties setting out from St. Leonard's House: men with hats and extravagant moustaches, boys in caps and knickerbockers, my grandfather's white walrus moustache marking out the middle, rather like a group photograph of a college. But I can only remember one of these in my time, and that had been something of a disaster: the gig, the picnic basket, and the guns had taken up position in a clearing in the woods near Wivenhoe; suddenly a rabbit had run into the open, and, hit, had jumped into the air, to fall in a small, bloody bundle. I had cried and cried, and was never again taken on one of these expeditions. The 'Divines', as I have said, were the old lady's preserve; they came to tea on Sundays, she went to tea at the Vicarage on Thursdays, Louisa's afternoon off. Sometimes my sister and I were taken, to the embarrassment of the Revd Mr Newcummen, who shied away from children, as he did from cats, with an almost visible shudder. But if we kept very quiet and sat very still, and did not spill, we were tolerated—and Canon Carter even *liked* children—and it was all well worth the effort at extra good behaviour and being dressed in a white silk shirt and velvet knickers, white socks, and black pumps, for there was always an array of tea-cakes, crumpets, muffins, buttered toast, sandwiches of half a dozen varieties, and very finely cut, white and brown bread and butter, a variety of jams, scones, cake with caraway seeds, chocolate cake and chocolate fingers, on little tables that fitted one above the other. The 'Divines' certainly made a big thing of tea.

Then there was old Mr Pawsey, the owner of the cattle-cake factory on the harbour and who had a lot of grown-up children. I am not sure of the exact status of Mr Townsend, the manager of the gasworks (that, with the prevailing wind from the east, could be smelt from the wood-shed at the bottom of the garden). Apart from the 'Divines', he was the nearest middle-class neighbour. Though my mother disapproved, my sister and I would jump at any opportunity to go and play in the Townsends' garden, which possessed a miniature tram, painted green, and with an open top, which could be pushed up a gradient, to the buffers at the far end of its rails, and which would then run down, almost at the clattering speed of the trams that came down Hythe Hill, stopping quite gently at its terminus, which had a real platform, just as the real tram stopped at its terminus, every twenty minutes, on the corner by the harbour.

Certainly, the old man had nothing against the Townsends, and the youngest son, Charlie, was his godson. At eight or nine, it was already apparent to me that my mother, who was the seventh child of a country doctor, had a more rigorous view of social relations and hierarchies than my Cobb grandparents. She even took against the miniature tram, saying that it was ostentatious and *nouveau*-something, that the Townsend children were spoilt. My grandfather had come up in business and had married well, but he was a simple, unpretentious man.

He met his fellow-Masons—he had been something important at the local Lodge, as well as at the annual Oyster Feast—at the Club, they did not come to the house. But my grandmother had a great many relations in the neighbourhood: Prested, White Colne, Halstead—the Hills were an extensive family—and these provided some of the sporting and shooting visitors. There were also regular visitors to the back door, especially in winter, with woeful tales, and generally accompanied by very ragged children, wearing old corduroy trousers, cut down to make rather long shorts, and held up by string, and with bare feet. These were always provided with small parcels of food, wood, and coal. A great many other small parcels went out into the Hythe with the gig. The old people were not blind to the extreme poverty of the neighbourhood; and 'Mrs Ma', in black silk and bonnet and veil, and Daisy, with her basket, had fixed hours and days for delivering these packets. Nor were they in the least resented by the local people. Fourteen or fifteen years after their death, visiting the Hythe while in the Army, I found them still spoken of, in the numerous pubs, with that uniquely English mixture of deference and local pride (the Hythe was very much a community, on the fringes of the town, and in an area which had grown around a still active port, open not merely to barge traffic, red-sailed, and to coasters, but also to boats from Denmark, with children on deck who had tow-coloured hair, the little girls in bright smocks and with their hair in plaits, my first 'foreigners', though they did not seem so, they were so very much part of the Colne; and there was a reminder of them, too, in the little church of Copford, where there was a portion of human skin under glass, allegedly of a Danish blasphemer, who had been skinned alive at some remote time, the skin in its frame the gift of a Nathaniel Cobb in the 1770s. So, what with the Colne and the village my grandfather had come from, Denmark seemed very close). 'They were real old-fashioned people, not at all stuck up, and very kind.' 'Old Mr Cobb used to stop for a word, every day.' 'The old lady never went out without her bonnet and veil.' 'You should have seen the gig, the paint on it *shone*.' Nor, so it seemed, had they ever *preached*. My grandfather was a drinking man; and living opposite two very rowdy pubs, the red curtains of their windows throwing a reddish glow over the middle of the hill, he took drunkenness and shouting and wild bouts of singing, especially at weekends, as part of the Hythe scene. He knew about Mills's drinking habits, and as long as they caused no grave damage to the horse or to the gig, he preferred to ignore them. Drunkenness was as much a feature of the steep hill as the muffin-man with his bell at 4 p.m., the organ-grinder with his monkey, the lamp-lighter with his long pole, and the brilliantly lit trams as they careered downwards to the river. My grandparents probably knew a great deal more about their neighbours than did the 'Divines', shut away in the Vicarage, the Revd Mr Newcummen even more cut off as one of the last surviving Tractarians. It would have been hard to imagine that fastidious, bewigged, starched, frilled, manicured, and powdered High Anglican not turning up his nose in distaste when confronted with the pungent (and most appetising) smell of cattle-cake emanating from the harbour, harder still to picture him picking his way down one of the narrow, filthy alley-ways that lead off the Hill, though the bald and rotund Canon Carter was no doubt much closer to his parishioners.

I think what impressed Mrs Steggles, the greengrocer, when I talked to her in 1943, was the fact that my grandparents had been so *old*, had lived so long in the Hythe, and had made so few concessions to changing tastes and fashions. They had stuck to the brightly painted, polished gig, my grandmother to bonnet and veil, black silk, and voluminous fur, my grandfather to high-winged collar, narrow jackets buttoned down, panama, and boots. Mills too, known in every pub, regularly dismissed—one could imagine him going into one of the pubs opposite, and saying: 'the Guv'nor has sacked me again'—and as regularly forgiven—had likewise become part of a local legend, embroidered perhaps to the extent of having him fall off his box, which he never did. The 'old people' had maintained their style of living to the very end, almost as an act of defiance, more likely because they knew no other, and possibly were as much conditioned by elderly servants, as their elderly servants were held in bondage to the rigid habits and timetable of their master and mistress. They made their regular appearances at regular times, on foot, or, together with Mills, in the splendid gig. They might shut themselves away within the house, *côté-jardin*, which was the chosen realm of sleep and daytime silence (there was little sleep, even for a child, on the street side, on a Saturday) or afternoon doze; but they did not draw their blinds on to the Hythe; and any passer-by, from the raised platform offered by the right-hand pavement, as one went down the hill, could look down into the dark, cool depth of the two front rooms, lit by a flickering fire that reddened the silver. Primus, at nearly seventy, was hardly more *modern* than his parents; and there was nothing *modern* about poor Daisy, who, at fifty or more, still wore the clothes that she had possessed at nineteen, at the time of the disaster to her parents; this was not in an effort to cling to a distant girlhood, but because the pocket money her uncle gave her was either not sufficient to invest in new clothes, or, more probably, was spent on cigarettes, choco-late, and sweets. Nor had there been anything *modern* about Daisy's upbringing; there was hardly anything that she could do for herself, she could not cook or sew, nor even make her bed (which, so my mother claimed, remained unmade for weeks; it may well have been so; but my mother was a harsh judge of Daisy, seeing in her the very figure of *sloth*, something that outraged her own industry and independence, displayed already in her twenties, when she had taken up a teaching post in a Boer school in Bloemfontein; she would frequently complain that her father-in-law was over-indulgent, and that Daisy should have been put to something *useful*, though it was hard to see what that could have been); she was extremely ignorant and was quite incurious, and her only social accomplishment was to be able to play the piano and to sing (so my sister tells me, for I never heard her do either; such activities must have belonged to the hidden world of 'after bedtime' when the port came out, and my grandmother and Daisy moved over to the garden side). Daisy's father had been a country solicitor; and Daisy had been brought up like a young Victorian middle-class girl: to do nothing other than wait for marriage. By the time I came along, she had long since given up waiting for that. All she waited for now was the next meal.

The landlords of the two pubs directly opposite, the Dolphin and the Green Dragon, could have regulated their watches from the different *entrées* and *sorties* to and from St. Leonard's House: Ellen, the first on the scene, at 7.30, shaking out the mat on to the street; Primus, very erect, collared-and-chained, on foot, with his stick and hat, at 10 sharp treble-checked (back at 10.20 sharp); Daisy, with basket, at 11.15 (back at 12.15, but not on the dot, she was not punctual, to change for lunch); the old man, driven up the Hill, to his club, at 3.30; Primus, out again, watch in hand, at 3.45, the second 20-minute walk, before returning to make the arrangements for his mother's tea, communicating her preferences to Louisa; the old lady, walking to the Vicarage, up the Hill, at 4 (a reminder that it was Thursday); at 6.30, the old man driven back, the gig put away, and the street entrance to the stable-yard closed, to be re-opened at 7 by Mills, on his first visit of the evening to the Dolphin, moving next door to the Green Dragon at 8.30, back to the Dolphin for an hour before closing time. Ellen would go home at 9. Nothing much would happen after that, though Mills presumably struggled back to his room over the stables at about 11.

Each of these figures was part of the landscape, indeed, *moving* figures, not static and long-legged, as in a Lowry painting; and each offered the living reassurance of continuity. Take one away, and the pack would be incomplete, so that the whole thing would break down. The old people were ninety-one, turning ninety-two, and ninety-three at the time of their deaths, within six months of one another. They had lived in the house for as far back as most people could remember. They had been there at the time of the Earthquake, when my father had been still a schoolboy at the Royal Grammar and had seen a steeple fall down on his way to the Lexden Road. They had been there at the time of the Jubilee, at that of the Boer War, the death of the Queen (my grandfather used to say that he could never get used to having a King), and in 1914, and they were still there in 1918. St. Leonard's House and the Hythe had been through a great many things together; and my grandfather had even provided the new bells for the church which had announced both the happier and the more sinister of these events. So it would have seemed a very long time indeed, probably as long as the unforgettable presence of the Revd Mr Newcummen, a sort of ecclesiastical *Dorian Gray*, fighting back against *les outrages du temps* under his red wig and his pomaded skin, which, close up, looked like the delta of the Bramaputra, dressed in the elaborate manner of a mid-Victorian High Churchman—although, in fact, they had only been in the house about sixty years at the time of their deaths in 1928. It was hard to say just when the Revd Mr Newcummen had turned up at the Vicarage, or what function he served there; but, again, for the Hythe, Canon Carter and the Revd Mr Newcummen, in that unchangeable order, had been like Tweedledum and Tweedledee, as far as memory went back. The Hythe seemed to favour couples and 'Charlie' and 'Mrs Ma' were a very loving, very devoted one; it was as a couple that they had thus presented the familiar reassurance of apparent permanence. It was merciful, to all concerned, that, after 'Charlie's' death, 'Mrs Ma' only lingered on for another five or six months, increasingly confused and wandering, her conversation harking back to people and places of the 1840s and 1850s, to Elizas, Prudences, Constances, and Adelaides, to Nathaniels, Ebenezers, Hyrams, and Isaiahs, whom she now took to be familiar to all around her, about whom she reminisced in the rather quavering voice of a young girl, and who could probably have been identified from the gravestones of the churchyards at Prested and White Colne. My sister and I have heard her thus rambling on, in between bouts of tears, among dead aunts and cousins and relatives never mentioned perhaps during the previous forty or fifty years, reaching back further and further in time, even before 'Charlie', when 'Charlie' was still in Copford, and when she herself had been a tall, strong, big-limbed young woman, in a large house in Prested, Colchester a place to visit for important shopping, the Hythe unthought of, her life ahead of her. It was merciful, so the older neighbours told me, that she did not have long to wait. And then, with her death, and as if in homage to the old couple, everything began to fall apart: the house, Primus, Daisy, Mills. Whether that other couple, the two 'Divines', left the Vicarage together, or whether the one survived the other, I do not know. But that is to look ahead. My grandparents had succeeded in immobilizing a community and a quarter in a period of time, as if one year would always be like the previous one, and as if the Hythe could somehow manage to live outside public history and the public calendar of catastrophe, defeat, victory, revolution, bloodshed, civil war, sedition, envy, rancour, cruelty, and violence, as long as the old regular movements went on and the blue gig with the beautiful yellow wheels made its regular appearances. Perhaps Primus's obsession with the exact time came from an obscure awareness that, as long as a strict daily routine was adhered to, things would go on as before. That, I think, is why so many people felt attached to the old lady and the old gentleman, and why, even as late as 1943, they were still remembered with a mixture of pride, affection, and wonderment.

The continuity of life above-stairs in St. Leonard's House was reflected by a similar continuity below-stairs. I have said that Mills was believed to have taken part in the Crimean War—something that is wholly possible, as he would then have been somewhere between sixteen and eighteen (he did not know his exact age, nor his place of birth). I think he must have been taken on by my grandfather in about 1890, to replace a groom called William. Ellen, the daily, had been coming since the turn of the century. Louisa, the house parlourmaid, a very good-looking, stately woman, had been engaged for seventeen years, 'walking out' with her 'young man' on Thursday afternoons (hence the tea at the 'Divines') and every other Sunday, washing and darning his socks and collars; she said that she would not leave 'the old lady' for as long as she lived (which was to ninety-three) and she only got married in 1929, a year after the old lady's death, when she was in her late forties and her 'young man' must have been topping fifty. I think such devotion and self-abnegation were by no means uncommon, and modern social historians would be mistaken to identify master–servant relations in stark terms of exploitation. It could not be said, for instance, that the old man exploited Mills, whose main function at least by the time I came on the scene, was to see that the mare got enough exercise to remain in good trim; both horse and gig had by then largely outlived their daily use, but, if they went, what was to become of Mills?

So they stayed, and uses—most agreeable ones for my sister and myself—were invented for all three (Jenny, Mills, and the gig). When I was very small, I was lifted up and strapped in the front, on the driver's seat, next to Mills, while my sister sat on the gun box at the rear end, facing backwards. Later, when I was considered safe, our positions were reversed; my sister thought it was grander and more dignified to face forwards, high up above the street and little low houses, high enough to be able to look into the bedrooms of the Hythe cottages (which looked rather like the fishermen's cottages on the flat coast). It looked even as if she were driving. I preferred the back seat, just as, later, I preferred the open back platform of Paris buses, as there is more truth in the street scene as it unwinds from the back: a vantage point that catches people unawares and in the belief that they are unobserved; how often, looking backwards, as the street drew away in reverse, would I see a small child in the process of picking its nose or surreptitiously pocketing an apple from a stall; whereas, from the front, people would behave as if they were in the path of a public procession, look up, even wave, or lift their caps. As a historian, it is still the gun-box seat that I prefer, surprising as it does people in intimacy, in unconscious private gesture, hunched up, or plunged in their own thoughts, slouching, their hands in their pockets, and spitting yellowish gobs of tobacco into the gutter. Furthermore, anywhere in the Hythe, but especially on the headlong downward slope towards the river, the gig would be followed by small groups of running barefoot boys and girls, the former holding up their baggy corduroys, calling out, in strident Essex, for chocolate, sweets, or even for the core of an apple, but, oddly (by present standards), never shouting abuse at the little creature perched up facing them.

The pretext for such daily excursions, generally at about mid-morning, was shopping. And my sister can recall an earlier time when the gig had actually stopped outside the fishmonger's in Head Street, and the fishmonger, in his blue-and-white striped apron and straw hat, had actually himself *come out into the street* and handed up the fish, which was then put into the box under the seat, wrapped around in ice and leaves. Then it would stop at the toy shop, which would engulf the little girl perhaps for as much as three-quarters of an hour, leaving Mills in charge of the horse, and unable to get down, at the end of which she would emerge with a twopenny set of coloured prints, used later, up in the front, for a game of Snap with the groom. But this conventional form of shopping had almost entirely ceased in my time, to be replaced by one which seemed to me quite mysterious. Mills would first head up the hill, stopping here and there at brightly painted pictorial signs: a black bull, a volunteer, a red cow, an eagle, an eagle and child, a dragon, a lion, a bear, a castle, cross-keys, a shield, a ship, an engine, a liner, a

27

plough, a moon, a half-moon, a sun with spikes around it, an oak tree, a man in profile wearing a funny hat, Queen Boadicea driving a chariot, a black boy, a crown. Mills would climb down, give the horse a nosebag of oats, and disappear inside. I could not make out what he *bought* in all these places, he never came out with anything, though his good humour seemed to increase with every stop, and so would the speed of our progress, so that, on the homeward down-hill run, we would be going at a fair gallop, and I would hold on to the railings round the back of the box with both hands. I was long puzzled by the apparent purposelessness of these often roundabout pictorial itineraries (in the course of which it would sometimes be necessary to double back in our tracks and return to a half-moon or a queen already visited, as if Mills had forgotten something there); but as they took us all over Colchester, even into the narrow streets of the Dutch Quarter, or past long brick walls of endless barracks, or past the house with bullet-holes in it, or in front of Mr Death's, the coal merchant, as there was always something new to look at from my high perch, while Mills was inside, and as Mills himself would be whistling quite merrily after the fifth or sixth stop, I thought this type of 'shopping' very much worthwhile.

So did my sister, out in the front. But then she was more directly motivated, as these excursions were accompanied by a game that, in addition to Snap, Mills and she used to play between stops: who could think of the names of twenty public houses? Then, thirty? Or even forty? Mills always won. Once, at lunch, unguardedly, she asked our grandfather why Mills was so much better at the game than she was. It was only after the purpose of these expeditions had been explained to me that I understood the full implication of my terrible gaffe on the subject of 'gee-gee falling down'. Even so, 'shopping' went on in this way till the deaths of the old man and the old lady. Jenny *had* to be exercised. It is true that Mills was also sent out on more specific errands, would meet the old man at the North Station (very prestigious, as *North* always is), St. Botolph's or the Hythe, if he had been away, or meet my mother at Hythe Halt, and would take the old lady out to the Lexden Road or to Mr Pawsey's house beyond the Clacton Road; but such missions were rare. He also took me out on foot, very early in the morning, to look for mushrooms (he called them 'rumes') in the fields around Wivenhoe Park. We nearly always came back with plenty. Mills was a man of many resources. He seemed to know the mushrooms as well as he knew a hundred-odd historical or allegorical signs. I never discovered if he were literate; but it has since occurred to me—as a result of working on late eighteenth-century French urban history—that he may have *read* his way across the town, from picture to picture, much as Parisian *commissionnaires*, laundresses, and servant girls guided themselves through the city from hanging emblem to hanging emblem: here a gigantic key, here a boot, here a yellow hat, here a flowing wig, there a vast spyglass, there a huge pair of scissors, there an inn-sign. But this is mere supposition. Ellen and Louisa could read; but Elizabeth, the cook, a tiny redhead from one of the Colnes, and who had been in service since she was nine, her parents happy to see her warm, clothed, and fed, could not. She too had been in the house for an unknown number of years, I don't think that she herself knew just how long. When my sister and I were staying in the house, coming over from Frinton, room would be found for our nannie: the first, Rose, who I think died of tuberculosis in 1916, the second Kate Scurrell, the eighth child of a country family from Great Holland, and who had somehow learnt to read and who later taught me my numbers.

For a small boy, from the rather hazy memory of three or four, to the much closer observation of eight to eleven, St. Leonard's House and the Hythe represented an ideal world of stability, predictability, and changelessness, as *solid*, as well-made, and as lasting as the objects on the tables or in the saddle-room, and in very marked contrast to the nomadic existence led by my parents, in between my father's periods of duty in the Sudan. St. Leonard's House was *home* and safety, Primus beating the gong gave the assurance of an unruffled future. Yet the safety provided by the high-walled garden and by the up-and-down house, with its creaking floorboards, its curved ceilings and sloping floors, its huge wood-encased bath and its generous wood-encased lavatories, the pans in pink and white patterns, by my grandmother's little silver wheelbarrow, used to contain peppermint creams, and by her teacups with violets, by her Barbary doves, and by the old familiar rich smells, and the changelessness of the daily routine were likewise illusory. There was a dreadful, hideous, inadmissible occasion when I was nine and when even the peace of the walled garden and the attempt to find reassurance in several bound volumes of nineteenth-century numbers of

Punch failed to drive away the awful memory of violence; Kate and
I had been for a walk beyond the Clacton Road, and, on the way
back, she had seen a crowd by the roadside, and I had followed her.
There had been a motor accident, involving a bull-nosed Morris: a
grey-haired woman laid out on the removed front seat, with trickles
of blood running from the corners of her mouth and her nose, her
face ashen, her eyes frightened and wide, a woman in a black dress
with blue and yellow flowers on it—a dress that I can still see, and
her shoes lying in the road, and one of her stockings coming down
almost to her knee: the next day I learnt that her name was Mrs
Elizabeth Knight, and that she had died in Colchester Infirmary; it
was in the *Essex County Standard*, which I read surreptitiously, at a
favourable moment between the first two breakfasts. I never told
anyone about the accident, partly because, if I had, Kate would have
been in trouble, as the Clacton Road was beyond the authorized
limits of our walks—the woodyards and sawmills on the other side
of the Colne and the fields near Wivenhoe Park—but mainly
because the evidence of death seemed to me something so completely inadmissible that I knew that neither my mother nor my
grandparents would ever be able to drive it away. I could not get the
colours of the dress out of my mind, and even the doves and the
walled garden were powerless. The Victorian calm had been
breached by 1926; and I never felt entirely safe again.

Two years later, the old people died, and Primus, at seventy, went
to live in a boarding-house, The Grange, in Clacton on Sea. At first,
it all turned out surprisingly well. Now he could take his two
twenty-minute walks on the Pier, which might have been designed
for him, timing himself, four times up and down, in his usual
long-legged stride. I have a photograph of him, looking the picture
of health, twirling his stick, and with a pipe in his mouth. But it did
not last; he was being persecuted by two old ladies, who, he was
convinced, wanted to marry him, and, worse, had designs on his
gold hunter. His complaints and fears got more and more strident;
in the end, my father had to go over, and have him driven from
Clacton to Severall's Hospital, where he died, in less than a year, of
senile dementia. It was the only time, apart from a year up the
Amazon, that he had been away from home, 'Mrs Ma' having
decreed, when he was twenty-one, that he was delicate. Poor Daisy
was found a room in the Hythe, down an alley off the hill, with a

woman who was paid to look after her, feed her, and see to her changes of clothing; but, losing all interest in life, and without her uncle to greet her in the morning, she soon took to her bed, and my father received a badly spelt letter in green ink, from the woman with whom she had been placed, to say that she had 'passed away quietly'. I am sure she did that, she had always tried not to be a nuisance; I think she died of loneliness and despair. But, as my mother said at the time: 'Where could *we* have put Daisy?' Louisa at last got married. Mills went into an old people's home and was kept in drink and tobacco by what my grandfather had left him. I believe he lived to almost a hundred. Ellen and Elizabeth got positions elsewhere. And we never went to the Hythe again, though, in 1943, when I was stationed at Dovercourt, I cycled over, visited Copford, and spent two nights in St. Leonard's House, sleeping on an Army camp-bed in my old bedroom next to the Ghost Cupboard. The house had been taken over by a Signals Unit; and the garden had grown quite wild, the dovecot was still there, but the greenhouse had lost most of its glass and was falling in. One could still pick out the pattern of flower-beds, and the graves of Tim-Tom and the old Labrador were still visible as slight mounds in the thick undergrowth at the far end near the rotting wood-shed. Only 'Mrs Ma's' geraniums, in their two stone pots, had prospered.

The Mill House

Anthony Thwaite

As if mine, not as owner, as if I built the place,
I show them round, friends, visitors, friends of friends:
Here the mill-cut, and here the Tudor brick
(So I repeat facts caught from learned folk),
And here the window-catches someone else
Assigned to 1720, more or less.
Notice the floorboards in this upper room—
Not later than the 1660s, so
Reliably I'm informed, and pass it on.

31

Six Houses

This wall must once have been an outer one,
Though now resolved into a late addition.
Everywhere has its date, its style, its place.

And then they go, and leave me here, to share
Something with every date, and style, and place,
An ownerless owner, moving towards a date
No one has told me of, or yet assigned.

Ryedale

Piers Paul Read

Are men like salmon who, however far they swim in the oceans of
the world, are drawn back to the streams where they were born? My
father's family farmed in Ryedale, that precious province of North
Yorkshire, hidden and protected by natural frontiers from the
outside world—to the north by the sharp escarpment of the Cleve-
land Hills and the purple waste of the North York Moors; to the
south and to the west by the Howardian and Hambleton Hills and
to the east by the North Sea—blank and empty, giving no sense of
anything on the other side.

Over a period of two hundred years, in the eighteenth and
nineteenth centuries, the family's fortunes rose from those of a
widow who grazed a single cow on the poor land beneath the moors
to those of a prosperous tenant farmer of the richer soil by the River
Rye seven miles to the south. My grandfather kept hunting horses
and his brother went to university at Cambridge, but in 1902 he
died; and since he had only been a tenant of someone else's land his
wife was obliged to sell the stock and move away with her three
sons. My father, Herbert Read, was sent to an orphanage in
Halifax; and at fifteen started work in a bank in Leeds. In 1914 he
went to fight in France; and after the war he lived in London,
Edinburgh, then London again until in search of country life he
moved to Seer Green in the Chiltern Hills. There he lived in a house

built to his own design; many friends lived nearby; but he was not content.

> Here where I toil from hour to hour,
> The folk are mean and the soil is sour,
> God grant that I may come to die,
> Between the Rickle and the Rye.

In 1949 he moved back to Yorkshire.

The house he chose was the Old Rectory at Stonegrave, a mile or two from the farm where he had been born. It was a larger, grander house built at the end of the eighteenth century for the younger son of a local landowner. The north side which faced the village was sober and forbidding as if a dour façade was expected of a clergyman: but the side which faced south over lawns to open countryside, hidden from public view by a belt of trees, was cheerful and voluptuous as if the owner, once down from the pulpit, could return to the life of a country gentleman.

Beside the house there was a large courtyard where once the rector's servants had gone about his business, with a barn, stables, two coach houses and numerous other outbuildings—one with an old copper boiler for washing the clothes, the other with an equally antique diesel engine to generate electricity. It was separated from the garden by a tall wall, built like the house of flaking, honey-coloured limestone. A door led through from one to the other: it opened between two laurel bushes which formed a dark, green tunnel between the domestic bustle of the yard and the garden's landscape of leisured calm. From a terrace of stone flags which ran the full length of the house, the lawn fell steeply to a flat rectangle of close-cropped grass—for bowls or croquet—and then fell again in a longer, gentler slope to merge over a ha-ha with the field. On each side of the lawn there was a border of flowers and shrubs; in the centre there were six rose-beds; and, half-way between the house and the ha-ha, a huge Californian spruce rose incongruously above the pink pantiled roofs where it had been planted to commemorate Wellington's victory at Waterloo.

Standing on the ha-ha one had a different view in each direction. To the south, across the field, there was a line of trees beside the stream which bordered our property and beyond that, in the

distance, the pine forest of the Howardian Hills. To the east, over
the roofs of the neighbouring farm, rose the tower of Stonegrave
Church. To the west was the line of beech, elm, and sycamore trees
which shielded the garden from the lane; and to the north was the
house itself—a bald green hill, tufted with trees, rising behind it.
From here it seemed like a little palace. The four long, languid
windows to the drawing-room stood to one side of the garden door:
the three shorter but equally elegant windows to the dining-room
were to the left, each one matched above by the windows to the
bedrooms on the first floor. The limestone walls were covered with
red and green creeper, and between each window there were separate pillars of honeysuckle, clematis and climbing roses.

Behind the windows the rooms were of an equal elegance, expressing in their proportions their architect's conviction that a man of
God may live pleasantly in this world and yet retain his expectations
for the next. A huge kitchen with arches over the ovens had been
built to cook abundant food; there was a barrel-vaulted cellar with
racks ready for the wine; and behind one of the shutters in the
dining-room was a concealed cupboard for a chamber-pot so that
those friends of the rector who remained with him to drink claret
on a winter's evening—after dinner when the ladies had withdrawn—should not be obliged to leave the room just to relieve their
bladders. My father liked to think that the two rectors of neighbouring parishes, Laurence Sterne and Sidney Smith, might once have
been guests at Stonegrave and that their cheerful spirits lingered in
the stone-flagged passages of the house.

In the early nineteenth century two wings had been added and it
was in one of these that my father made his study. A large, north-
facing room was lined with books and adorned with a few favourite
works of those modern painters he had fortuitously collected. The
room was dark and looked on to the village street: he said he did not
want to be distracted from his work by the beauty of the view to the
south, but in that room itself he created a beauty which was not in
any of the pictures or the furniture, nor in the fastidious arrange-
ment of the books and small works of art, but in the atmosphere of
enquiry, concentration, and learning. Just as in the garden you
met different scents from the different flowers, so in the study the
eye ranged over the volumes of poetry, drama, philosophy and
psychology and the mind's nose sniffed the names of Jung, Herzen,

34

Cervantes, Eliot, Conrad, Piaget, Nietzsche, William and Henry James. The study, like the house itself, was a secret kingdom within the secret kingdom of Ryedale. It was the fortress of a man who had decided that reality lay in the mind and the imagination.

My father lived on his salary from a London publishing house, and on what he earned by writing books and lecturing on art. From this he had to meet the expenses of a house which was built to be run by half a dozen servants. The garden alone was work for three men. My father employed one who did what he could to encourage some plants and discourage others; but such was the richness of the soil that no sooner was the weather warm than mongrel weeds would push from the ground and the grass start its relentless sprouting on the lawn. To control this chaotic fecundity was more than one man could do. The lawn was mown each week, and the weeds in the flower garden were kept at bay, but by July the vegetable garden was largely overgrown—the strawberries strangled by couch-grass, the gooseberry bushes lost altogether in an impenetrable jungle of nettles, elderflower, thistles, and bindweed.

This degeneration into a wilderness of a once orderly garden might not have mattered if my father had been a less fastidious man; but he liked everything in order—the row of bright bow-ties in his dressing-room, the papers on his desk—and he suffered to see the weeds triumph over the flowers, fruit and vegetables. He was equally pained by the slow disintegration of the house itself. Each winter the rain would soak into the porous limestone—then freeze, expand, and crumble the fabric. Slowly the gentle façade of the house had been pitted by this process until the lintels over the windows were cracked, and small blocks of masonry were only held to the wall by the tendrils of the creeper.

Most of my father's day was spent working in his study. At weekends he might drive up into the Moors or to the ruined abbey at Rievaulx, or he would walk along the ridge of Caukleys Bank with its views over Ryedale to the scenes of his childhood. The buildings and landscape were all that remained from his past. No close relatives remained in Ryedale and he made no attempt to befriend the kind of man his father must have been. Life had taken him far from the habits and customs of a Yorkshire farmer. Moreover he was shy and had returned to Ryedale to escape from people—importunate abstract painters and unpublished poets. He was convinced that he could be content with his family and his books but he sorely missed a Laurence Sterne or Sidney Smith. Their ghosts were not enough and often, especially in winter, a melancholy boredom would come over him for days on end.

Yet he never regretted his return to Ryedale. Whenever he came back from some journey—either to London, or further afield to Australia, America, China or Japan, he would sit on the stone-flagged terrace looking down the lawn to the line of trees by the stream and swear that nowhere on earth was there a more beautiful view than that from his own garden.

In July 1968 he died in a bedroom which overlooked the terrace. His shrouded body lay for a while in our drawing-room; then the coffin was closed and it was taken from Stonegrave over Caukleys Bank, across the River Rye and the River Riccal, past Nunnington where he had first gone to school and Muscoates where he had been born, to be buried near his father's grave at Kirkdale—the church where he had worshipped as a child.

Guma's Valley

RONALD BLYTHE

I was about to begin, 'I remember my first sight of this remote old house', only to realize that I do not. It is a wholly unexpected realization. Does it mean that, from now on, I must assume some loss of recall of what happened at the beginning of things, and that I could be one of those people who fail to stock up naturally with initial impressions, whether of places or people? The notion that my brain doesn't start its docketing processes until the importance and necessity of someone or something in my life has been confirmed by subsequent encounters, is a novel one. But a few tests prove the opposite, and so it is just this farmhouse. There was a day when I first saw it, but the day has got lost and since diary-keeping has always been a stop-go affair with me, and those who lived here then had no reason at that time to put me in their journals, no words exist to jog my memory. It would have been summer, certainly, which may be why, even in bare and open January, the site for me retains an all-the-year-round seclusion and density. I never so much as come back from a walk without feeling that I have to break my way into it, although winding grassy paths give access in all directions.

My old friends John and Christine Nash bought it for a few hundred pounds in the middle of the last war. It was quite in character that although he was busy in the Marines and she working endless hours at different ports, there should run parallel the dominant peace-time obsessions of a home from which one need never walk more than half a mile to find plenty to draw and paint, and a garden in which there was a soil for all seasons. They'd actually had their eye on it for a decade or more before they took the plunge and took it off Mr Lewis's hands, as they said. He must have given one of those great heartfelt sighs of agricultural relief, for it had been empty for years and was rapidly becoming, in the way of ancient dwellings of its kind, all of a hummocky, bosky piece with its grounds. Nettles (which always grow at their mightiest best where men have lived for generations) grew all around it by the acre, and fruit trees had impacted themselves with the architecture, so that here and there one could reach up in a room and pick Blenheim Oranges or elderberries. And just as there were boughs trying to get indoors, so there were writhing hanks of convolvulus doing their best to get out. After all these years one still finds a few inches of it curling from the crevasses in the scrubbed floor where the patterns created by moist clay set out to dry on Stuart or Georgian grass show up vividly after a dose of Flash. Brick-floor scrubbing is, of course, a lost art—and a well-lost art at that, most will say. But the colour it brought to the interiors of all sorts of buildings, churches, inns, farms, and cottages, used to be an important element in their aesthetic. The brick floors in this house don't stay wet and brightly coloured for more than an hour or two. One has hardly had time to put the rugs back before the little flattened shapes of plants of centuries ago vanish from their fast-drying surfaces and they take on their parched, anhydrous look, clinking silverly where they are loose. When John and Christine took the house on (I use this phrase judiciously, for its ownership involves one in a running battle of wills between occupier and half a millennium of local building materials) the stream actually ran straight through it, like the stream in Wordsworth's Dove Cottage. It is a few yards to the north of the garden now, I'm relieved to say, but still part of the watery network which culminates in the slow-flowing Stour, Gainsborough's and Constable's river only a mile or two off. At certain moments when the light is caught, this famous river, one of whose little arteries enticed a Saxon farmer to chance his luck in this spot, glitters and winks against the windows, and the sound of the stream running to it never ceases. Neither ice nor drought has ever silenced it.

Although the house had suffered some of the typical vicissitudes of the agricultural depression, having its hundred or so acres annexed by a neighbouring farm, coming down in the world from yeoman independence to squire's tenantry and even to becoming a double-dweller for farm-workers, and ultimately to years of empti-ness, it had never been entirely abandoned, for I recently discovered the following pencilled on the inside of a 'Tenner' cigarette-box which had been carefully placed on a ledge under the stairs: 'Feb 19th 1937 painted outside of this House and Distempered inside. H. W. Spooner and B. Welford. NAYLAND & Boxted.' The box also contained a nail and a hazel-nut. But the abandonment of its ancient roadway, barns, piggery and stackyard was another matter. There had been no attempt to keep these in some ticking-over order, and from being the means of access and operation of the place, they had, with astonishing swiftness, reversed their roles and become the chief threat to its future habitation. There is almost no more daunt-ing ruin than a ruined farm, or a more unappealing one. The merciful thing was that neither John nor Christine would have seen the place in such terms. Its past and future laid lightly on their conscience and imagination. They simply had an exciting hunch of the uses it could be put to *now*, even in the middle of a war, and in this respect they were like that great seventeenth-century gardener John Tradescant who, while fighting in a battle, was observed botanizing during the carnage, bending down among the swords and blood and digging up interesting specimens. And so they spent the latter part of their work-filled lives here, and myself the first part of mine. These years running away from and towards the centre have passed slowly and thoroughly, leaving parallel but differing impressions. For quite a long time after their deaths I felt it a compulsion and a duty to let things run on in the way they always had, and which they could have done, because strong personalities and well-regulated lives leave behind them rhythms and patterns which have learnt how to repeat themselves long after those who originally set them in motion have departed, but one morning this need simply wasn't there. It had evaporated, had been overcome like the hoar-frost hanging around in the frost-pocket by the bay-tree when the sun burst in on it.

It is always a problem to know what to do in a landscape where others have done so much. Do nothing, could be the answer. It is finished, so contemplate on what is. But gardens and antiquated water supplies, and banks and medieval tracks, not to mention the view itself, partly exist to keep one on the go, physically and intellectually, and the mere maintenance of what 'is' subtly turns it into what you would like it to be. I doubt if one could so much as weed a bed without leaving one's own creative mark. Not that such minimal activity would have done for Bottengoms, or Guma's Valley, where I have an increasing sense of its inhabitants being kept well on the go for centuries. A closer stare at its situation tells me that the farm crouches sideways in a valley which is in a valley, that ages ago the people who worked here dug out a shallow recess in the western hill so that they could dwell in a high-rimmed saucer lowered into the natural declivity. And more digging on an heroic scale must have gone on between the front garden and the first of the front fields, where one side of the ditch is as steep as a defensive earthwork. The up-hill, down-dale of it all makes it laborious still. Nowhere can one see everything at once; it is all vistas within vistas and, from less than a mile off, even these interlocking definitions vanish and last winter, plunging back from the village along the field ridges where the snow was thinnest, I found to my amazement that Guma's half-dug, half-natural valley had utterly disappeared in a white-out and that a compass wouldn't have come amiss. On that icy day I understood an important aspect of the farm's siting where John was concerned, how its landscape was both domestic ('Back to the old homestead!' he would say as his little car, crammed with drawing-boards, bottles of milk, fishing-tackle, plants, and plenty of rubbish, jogged down the track) and dramatic. How its solid 'peace', as the visitors invariably describe its atmosphere, is for its residents shot through and fractured by sharp little threatenings which you can't actually put your finger on but which keep you on

The Barn at Bottengom's Farm by Charles Hall

your toes. Low-lying places are supposed to be soporific but this sunken house isn't. Cunningly masked by an extravagant display of calm, it has its own uneasy system of alerts to raise the adrenalin.

It could be the valley's objection to the hubris which has unconsciously beset its most recent occupancy. All this painting and writing, it is saying, what does it amount to in my time-scale? Forty years of art as against possibly fourteen hundred years of ploughing, of centuries of feeding off those slopes which provide only your views. Even in your present house, the valley insists, men and women have been looking out of the windows since the Tudors, and seeing much the same folds and clefts in the soil, and their accompanying skies, and it is likely that not a fraction of what you say you see so much as crossed their minds. Rooms, grounds, the stream, the track, how can they be expected to run without protest to these come-lately rhythms after running for such ages in time with the great drudge of the seasons?

There scarcely exists so much as a pencil scrawl of the house itself by John. Every kind of oil, water-colour, drawing, and woodcut of everything spread out around it, of course, but not of the building itself. Its purpose for him was to be able to work away inside it at what he could see from it. Like the subjects people never mention, there is a special eloquence about this deliberate omission. What was it about the house that forbade him putting it into the picture? The barns, yes (the last tumbledown skeleton of which is being battered into the earth by tractors as I write), the basic lines of Guma's land certainly, for such patterns provided him with a kind of ultimate poetry; every tree, every cutting and, if he could have had his way, every flower, but not the old homestead, a phrase often said in a tone of cagey mockery.

It is a beautiful house, powerful, confident. It is a typical East Anglian long house which likes you to think that it is younger than it is and no more than three or four hundred, but tucked away under its artful bodging lurks its true antiquity. But it follows the traditional style of a huge rectangular oaken frame set on brick sills, and with the interstices of its half-timbering (halved or cut wood, as opposed to unshaped logs) stuffed tight with wattle screens plastered with earth. The roof is its crowning glory without a doubt. Originally thatched and dizzily steep, it has since the eighteenth century boasted one of the most generous tile slopes in the neighbourhood, for after the addition of the Georgian dairy and store-rooms its descent was carried to within four feet of the garden. These lovely hand-made tiles in their many thousands, and some still pinned to the battens with delicately whittled hawthorn pegs, do not descend with a sheer, hard linear force, but with a slightly dipping, skirt-spreading concavity which is so gentle that one doesn't notice at first that there is such a lovely tilting check in their rush towards the grass. The rooms ramble into each other with a not so much as 'by your leave' and have never heard of anything as discreet as a corridor. Here and there are fragments of generations of partitioning, shoved up and pulled down as many now unknowable births and deaths required. In the roof itself, and quite window-less, but still white- and blue-washed, are a lot of little rooms which can only be reached by ladders, and which could have been the bothy, or the unmarried labourers' quarters. Straw pallets, snow on their faces, and mouse fidgetings. Downstairs the vast open hearths still hide behind a Victorian grate and an oil-fired Rayburn respectively. The latter is very near to being the house-god, so comfort- and pleasure-giving is it. William Barnes once wrote a furious and despairing poem about the usurpation of the ancient hearths by the Rayburn's nineteenth-century ancestors.

The garden surges urgently against the walls and has to be beaten back. In summer the south wall completely vanishes behind a thirty-foot vine in which birds sleep in their scores. One hears their weary flittering and cheeping just behind the bedhead, and when there is a strong wind, the scrunch of vine boughs on the brickwork. The vine is so high that I've never managed to get at the topmost grapes and they swing just below the apex of the roof until November, when they tumble, soft and rotten, into the huge euphorbias which flourish here. Dioscorides, who was physician to Antony and Cleopatra, and who also wrote one of the first herbals, is said to have named this great spurge after Euphorbus, physician to King Juba of Mauritania. John considered it 'very handsome', an accolade he bestowed on women as well as favoured plants. Along the dairy wall and recessed between fat brick buttresses are fuchsias and, in late summer, a forest of balsam whose seed-pods explode at the merest finger-touch, communicating their own urgency to the human nervous system. *Impatiens*, the botanists call it. The saucer-shaped ground tips sharply upwards here and the garden John made loses itself in the Old Orchard, a tangled, fruitless place which is a rabbit and pheasant kingdom, and from which one bursts on the far side upon a soaring view that encompasses Bures and the landsweep towards Aga Fen. This is East Angle—East Saxon border country where King Edmund was crowned in 855. He was fifteen and he reigned for fifteen years before the manner of his death turned him into England's St. Sebastian. I can see Cuckoo Hill, the site of his coronation, from the garden-edge, as well as the smudge of brown which is Bottengom's Farm from the spot where Edmund, Offa's adopted son, received the Saxon diadem. The Stour divides these tribal lands. Its name means 'powerful' or maybe 'worshipful stream' and perhaps there is a mystic connection between this lovely Suffolk–Essex river and the River Stura in Cisalpina Gallia which flowed near the Rubicon and into Italy to join the Po. These classical thoughts are allowable to someone living in an old valley only six miles from Colchester, the birthplace of St. Helena, mother of Constantine, the shrine of the deified Claudius—and the capital of Cymbeline. Our church tower is entirely built of Roman bricks, and as children we searched for arrow heads on the hillside below Edmund's chapel as this particular field was said to be where Boadicea skirmished, although we never found one. The harvests from Bottengom's would have floated slowly past it on the river barges which collected up produce from Harwich to Sudbury. My neighbour who has farmed the Bottengom's fields for fifty years tells me that deep in the chalk of those which rise so spectacularly to meet one's gaze as one clambers from the Old Orchard, there are seven springs. One of them has 'watered' this place ever since it was inhabited, man and creatures. The others break surface further along in ponds, a small lake, ever-running ditches, and cuts.

John loved a pond as much as anything. 'Never pass up a good pond', was his motto. The four in his garden are tiny but crammed with fish and plants. In the summer you need a machete to find them. The boggy ground near them produces an heroic vegetation, partly exotic, partly native, which totally conceals them. In the old days there would be pond-cleaning forays when the weather was hot so that we could work in them stripped except for a thin, silky covering of mud, and with the perch darting between our knees. 'It's clean mud', we told each other as we dragged up the weed. He often painted these ponds in their catholic thickets of bamboo, crab-apple, giant dock, guelders, willow, and hemlocks. Nightingales would sing there as he drew, though these have gone now.

To the east the garden is bordered by the track, the bastion-like entrenchment, and the pastures—now in the process of being ploughed for corn. Above this hill are the Horkesleys, the 'hurks' or Saxon lamb shelters, and a mysterious fortification called Pitchbury Ramparts, and below the hill on the other side lies the little wool town of Nayland whose bells and church clock can be heard in the farmhouse when the wind is right. A huge palette-shaped bed crammed to the edges with pink and yellow peonies, carpets of cyclamen, tea-roses and a lifetime's amassing of flowers of every kind is spread out here. I have sometimes seen friends or visitors attempting to formulate or diagnose what taste or impulse lay behind the creation of this garden, and I myself found it hard to say what judgement and rules made it and governed it. Until, after John's death, I began to read Dean Hole. Although in his enchanting *Book About Roses*—which I commend to anyone who is interested in pure pleasure—S. Reynolds Hole deals only with this supreme flower, I recognize both in accent and attitude a concept of gardening lust and philosophy, aesthetic and preferment which was John's to a T. It was an entirely unselfconscious, really wholly unaware Victorian standard of intellectual gardening that he introduced to Guma's midden and cabbage-patch, and maintained. Guma's garden, if such an unlikely thing existed, would certainly have been succeeded by a long list of country gardens with their matter-of-fact mixing of blooms and food, all different, all gone, save in remnants such as the great Portugal quince with its regular hundredweight of furry-skinned fruit and its not-quite-nice scent. Village folk used to add quince to an apple-pie to make it 'brisk', and they set it among their pear-trees to make them extra fruitful. It is very acid and maybe the pectin called quin is named after it. Fragments of old walls, too, circumscribe earlier garden patterns. And there is a stout holly hedge, half veiled in bryony, which was planted as a barrier against something or other long ago—though what? Lightly digging in the early spring, I now and then exhume a yard or two of the cinders and flints of Victorian paths. There remain, too, inconclusive stumps in the blond aftermath of rough scythings where fine old trees once stood, and which seem to petrify and remain, rather than rot away. John drew out the present garden above or around all this, as well as in terms which owed nothing to mid-twentieth-century taste in such matters.

He himself illustrated many excellent gardening essays by some of the best garden-makers of his time but the emotion or spirit of his own garden derives from the immediately preceding taste. And where is this taste most confidently and unaffectedly displayed—but in Dean Hole's *A Book About Roses*. Once, wandering about Falmouth, I stumbled across, as they say, the Dean's autobiography, *Then and Now*, which I triumphantly presented to John. He received it with the caution which one would show at being offered a key to what one has always privately known, and I was reduced to reading my own gift, though allowed to 'call bits out' (which he rather liked).

'Call a bit out', he'd say.

The bits I'd call out now would not be from the Dean's life, sensible and kind though it was, but from his little masterpiece, for if the essence of what occurred during the 1940s and '50s in Guma's Valley can be found on any printed page, it lies in this Victorian rosarium. John's pencil ticks against his favourite blooms in the appendix—*Charles Lefebvre*, *Mrs John Laing* ('a continuous bloomer'), *Prince Camille de Rohan* ('the freest flowering of all the dark roses'—he had a passion for dark roses), *Cristata*, *White* (Provence roses), *De Meaux* (miniature Provence or pompon), *Red Damask*, *Rosa Mundi*, and *Tuscany* (adored), *Boule de Neige* (dazzling white clusters), *Dundee Rambler* (Ayreshire), the creamy *Félicité Perpétué*, which is an evergreen, the *Old Blush* and *Cramoisie Supérieure* china roses, the great tea-roses *Bouquet d'Or* and, of course, *Gloire de Dijon* (his favourite flower) and the pretty little Japanese picotee-edged rose *Fimbriata*, all beloved roses of the Nineties, and most could have been found in Benjamin Cant's celebrated nursery at Colchester at this time—reveal his determination to collect those necessary for his existence, but it is the actual style and philosophy of the Dean's outlook on gardening generally which is echoed at Bottengom's. How amazed the previous owner, Mr Lewis, and indeed all those centuries of farmers and their wives who 'like to see a bit of a show, like, near the house' would have been by what John Nash liked. Winding, irregular paths, particularly with plants flopping over the edges, secret dank corners, walks mown between tall grass in which a sequence of flowers appeared from February to November, everything from precious things such as fritillaries and martagon or Turk's cap lilies, to lords and ladies, and especially handsome stands of sheep's parsley, and dead trees clothed in climbers. Wildness and cultivation were lured into hobnobbing.

The only way in which this early and this belated Victorian gardener differed entirely was in their botany. John called himself an artist-plantsman, not a gardener, the Dean a rosarian—and 'a true gardener'. John was also a brilliant botanist but the Dean, because he could not master the subject himself, doubted if one could find 'a scientific botanist and a successful florist [i.e. grower of flowers] under the same hat'. The Dean said he was like the undergraduate who, told off by a farmer for riding over his wheat, answered, 'I am no botanist'. So that while the Bottengom's garden is, in summer, knee-deep in those delights recommended by Dean Hole, it also contains a certain intellectual force which is not exactly relaxing. Except for eating his meals in it during good weather, I never saw John lying about on the grass, as I do. It kept him very much on his toes. The Dean, I fancy, would have been neither learned nor idle but would have walked about from shrub to shrub, joyful and exclaiming. Guma, should he catch sight of either one of us from his forgotten barrow on some stony hoo by the river, would be bewildered by the elaboration of it all. He who had the sheltered corn slopes, the beasts in the hurk, the running water, and the wooden hall to live in.

THE KINGDOM OF
THE SHORE

When I have seen the hungry ocean gain
Advantage on the kingdom of the shore,
And the firm soil win of the watery main,
Increasing store with loss, and loss with store . . .

SHAKESPEARE, Sonnet LXIV

Hamnavoe

GEORGE MACKAY BROWN

It falls sheer into the waters of a voe, the granite hill.

Twice a day the waters of the voe shift: they throb and brim and gleam; they ebb, leaving a desolation of stones and seaweed.

The hill faces east. Its hard outcrops catch glittering the first sun rising over Orphir.

Two small green islands form the other arm of the bay. The tide pours in from Hoy Sound, they are brimming islands in the flood. (But in the ebb a man can walk from island to island to island.)

The long blue tongue of the voe makes gentle utterances of fulfilment and desolation.

To the south rise two blue round scarred hills, Hoy.

And this beautiful enclosed voe was once a desolation.

Once the ice retreated and tribes began to move northwards, the shore under the granite hill cannot long have remained empty.

If they had knowledge of boats and fishing and sheltered places, the voe between the hill and the two green islands must have seemed a useful place and a beautiful place. (In those times—indeed, until comparatively recently—a man would not have distinguished between the useful and the beautiful.)

The new waters after the ice teemed with whales and lobsters and cod. The ice-sculpted hills swarmed with birds, the burns with trout.

It was not a bad place, that group of islands, for a tribe to settle and build, work, and legislate and breed, worship and dance.

Did the first-comers call the group 'whale islands'? Later settlers did. The name remained, while the waves of conquest went over: Picts, Norsemen, Scots.

Orkney.

Early Orcadians left great monoliths and stone burial chambers and stone villages behind them.

Other tribes left primitive stone keeps, 'brochs', along the shore: to deter their questing land-hungry cousins from southern Britain.

The Kingdom of the Shore

The Norsemen told stories. Their words, frail felicities of breath, have depicted a way of life more powerfully than the hewn stones: the behaviour of men fated and free.

But what storyteller wastes his breath on a few fisherfolk and their boats and lines and bothies between a granite hill and two green islands?

Even the little monastery two miles to the west is not worth a sagaman's harp-strokes. (The monks have their own seamless garment of psalms.)

But in the Norse castle on the other side of the bay there was a siege: battery and fire and flung insult. And one of the besieged ran all the way to Kirkwall fifteen miles away, and didn't stop until the shield on his back wedged in the great door of St. Magnus Cathedral there.

So the place finds a few heroic words in the *Orkneyinga Saga*.

The Norsemen called it Hamnavoe ('the haven inside the bay').

And the nameless unsung fishermen fished the dangerous waters under Hoy and Yesnaby. And the keeper of the castle set his few bondmen to plough the fields around.

So it went on for centuries.

The Scots gradually took over from the Norsemen. The *Saga* is changed to drab entries in business and legal documents.

One of these documents tells us that, in the last years of the sixteenth century, leave was given to a man called William Clark and his wife Mareon to build an inn at the very tip of the voe, the blue tongue.

These are the first recorded townsfolk.

Would William and Mareon Clark want to build an inn for a few poor fishermen and crofters, who kept their cupboards and ale-kirns privately plenished (if meagrely enough, sometimes)?

The shrewd eye of William Clark had seen how merchant ships were growing in size and venturesomeness from year to year.

Not the old tired trade routes of Europe would do for the new breed of skippers and merchants. They looked for the fabulous riches of Virginia and Newfoundland.

Often enough, between the North Sea and the Atlantic, those ships were storm-stayed in the Orkneys; and one of the safest harbours was the long blue tongue of sea between the granite hill and the little green islands.

54

No doubt ships poorly victualled with salt meat, hard bread, foul water, were glad enough to buy William's chickens, sides of bacon, new crisp bannocks, fresh-caught haddocks and lobsters, a barrel or two of Mareon's ale.

The trade grew and flourished.

Soon it was time for the hamlet of fishermen, Hamnavoe, to grow rapidly into the trading village called Stromness. The shrewd Orkneymen saw no reason why they too, should not lay keels and get rich on the fragments that fell from Baltic and American marts and exchanges.

Their problem was, how to build decent houses into the side of that implacable hill; how to have sheds and yards accessible to the sea.

Again, taking no thought for beauty but only for utility, they dug their granite foundations and they built stone piers (between a dozen and a score) out into the shifting waters of the voe. Their hundreds of houses were crammed between the salt and the granite; and among the houses uncoiled and twisted and surged the most unpredictable street in northern Europe.

We see it now as beautiful, the little town that had its best and richest and most storied time in the eighteenth century, when portentous figures—Alexander Graham, John Gow the pirate, George Stewart the *Bounty* mutineer, Bessie Millie the spaewife who sold good winds to skippers—moved among the piers and closes.

For them, hunger and poverty were still vivid enough to preclude ideas of beauty. The town and the harbour would do at last; it was serving its purpose; it was bringing in, to some, a modest affluence. It was a place to eat and love and sleep and trade in; a crazy little stone labyrinth, at best.

We come much later.

We had no part in the sweat of granite, sweat of shore stones, sweat of silver; in the dust of ledgers; in tarring and caulking, in a battle-scorched wall; in a tiny bell heard, westwards, between two waves.

We see this town, in the mathematical aridities of the new urban architecture, as an enchanted stone web.

Portknockie

RUSSELL HOBAN

Like the fungal hyphae that anchor lichens to rock there are ideas all dense and intertwined that grip us to the rock of existence; one of them is the idea of return, the idea that something once seen can be returned to significantly. What was seen, what might be the significance? We don't know, we are uncertain, we want to go back for another look.

In 1967 I saw Portknockie; in 1979 I wanted to see it again. All places begin with a night journey; I booked a sleeping compartment on the *Aberdonian* departing King's Cross 22.15, arriving in Dundee 09.15. Having been invited by a university I was going to Dundee to talk; having been invited by silence and the remembered wind I was going to Portknockie to listen.

Portnockie, with its idea of return beating in it like a heart, is itself an idea that beats like a heart in the larger body of things: it is the idea of living on the sea, by the sea, for the sea, and with the sea; it is the idea of getting a living and a dying from the sea, of continuing seaward and seawise regardless. A rocky shore of red cliffs, green humps and hillocks, shags and gulls above the green and marbling water foaming in among the names and bulks of landmarks: Green Castle, Port Hill, Bow Fiddle, rising from the sea. Dark and urgent the shags fly with long necks extended. The dark wings on the downstroke make an upside-down V; on the upstroke a right-side-up V; the downstroke and the upstroke make a dark X through which the body of the bird shoots like an arrow. The gulls descant above the foam and spray, their voices topographical, like contour lines in the air. The luggers are gone, the herring are gone.

The idea of Portknockie ascends from the simple geometry and arithmetic of its harbour, a tested formula that is like a spell, like words of stone and concrete to shelter boats from the sea: the breakwaters of the outer harbour and the inner harbour; the outflung arm of another breakwater beyond the outer harbour; the gaps where the boats pass from the wildness to the calm.

The houses of Portknockie rank themselves with thrifty slates above the harbour, like a congregation whose altar is below them.

The Kingdom of the Shore

The top floor of the Hythe Hotel affords a view of the sea with chimney-pots and starlings in the foreground. The window of the hotel room and the hotel itself are not known to me as I think about Portknockie in the sleeping-car, as I think about Portknockie in my little onward cabin of night. By day the towns we pass will be distinct and individual; by day the towns and places may or may not be of the present moment; but by night, dark trees against the sky or clustered lights they are all one thing, they are of the night and in the night belong at once to memory.

Having talked in Dundee I went to listen in Portknockie. I hired a car and headed north. At Montrose I turned north-west into the Grampians and the Cairn o' Mount road. Early May this was, wood-sorrel and primrose in the woods to the south. Over the mountains hung a blue-grey rain curtain against which soared white gulls. The rain once entered became sleet and snow. Winter abated and revealed a cruising owl low above the heather. People talk lightly of owls, poets have them for their stock-in-trade but other than in zoos I've only seen three owls in my life and this was the third: a tawny owl with a proper flat owl face on the front of it like a scanner in the clear grey air over the heather and the sedge at half past four in the afternoon. Coming out of the mountains I see, far from any strand, an oyster-catcher sitting on a post. The car passes within a few feet of it but it doesn't move until I turn and come back for another look, then it flies slowly away. And all of this is on the way to Portknockie, Portknockie hasn't happened yet.

When I come out of the mountains I feel an easing of tension; my relief shows me how much stronger than I knew was my craving for the open and the sea.

Then there is Portknockie and the top-floor hotel window with its view of chimney-pots, starlings, and sea: unknown in the sleeping-car but known now. Now with two large gins in me I roll pleasantly down Victoria Street towards the headland called the Green Castle. Knowing as I go that the idea of return may be wholly an illusion, that return may not be possible at all. Knowing that place itself may not be possible at all, that all the place there is may well be no more than the moving point of consciousness in us, that looking in its cage of bone that looks out through our eye-holes.

Then there is the sea, the green and marbling, the foaming and the milky water beating on the rocks and clattering the beach stones in

Skerray, Sutherland by John Blakemore

its backward suck, the stones that click and clatter under my feet. Bones there are too, sea-bones rounded by the grinding tidewash and the stones: bones of what? Sheep, cattle, dogs? I don't know. But place is possible, and return; even a moon, a little misty moon. I find myself saying, 'Ah! Ah! Ah! I'm so glad!'

Why such gladness? I don't know why Portknockie should have any special significance for me. When I was there twelve years ago I was writing copy for a scotch whisky; my companions were an art director and a photographer. I climbed the Green Castle; I was shown brown photographs by an old fisherman; I was not aware that anything in particular had happened. The place stayed in my mind and pulled me back to it. What is this idea of return? To what am I returning that I should exclaim with gladness? I don't know, I can't say. How does it feel then? 'It is a movement and a rest.' Those words describe it accurately; they are from Logion 50 of the Coptic *Gospel of Thomas* found at Nag Hammadi in Upper Egypt in 1945:

Jesus said: If they say to you: Whence have you come?, tell them: We have come from the light, the place where the light came into being through itself alone. It [stood], and it revealed itself in their image. If they say to you: Who are you?, say: We are his sons, and we are the elect of the living Father. If they ask you: What is the sign of your Father in you?, tell them: It is a movement and a rest.*

The last line of Logion 50 is for me the very essence of return; not so the lines leading up to it: the sea, the strand, the shapen rocks and headlands are not, for me, of the Father and the light but of darkness and the Mother—the Old Mother, Great Mother, Mother Goddess, womb of everything and nurturing body of earth.

Still, why the gladness? Returning to the womb of sea and darkness would be death and not yet welcome to me; this gladness is a lively feeling. I think it may be that emanations of origin make us glad, that we are glad to recognize in movement and in rest the womb of all motion, the genetrix of that potential energy from which the spark jumps at conception to begin the last stage of the night journey that brings us to the place of birth.

Just as the dome of St. Paul's Cathedral has its Whispering

* *New Testament Apocrypha*, Volume One, edited by E. Hennecke and W. Schneemelcher. English Translation edited by R. McL. Wilson, SCM Press Ltd, 1963.

Gallery that transmits sound, just as wet weather holds and intensifies smells, so the topography of Portknockie's shapen humps and
stony hollows, the rise and fall of its ground, holds, intensifies, and
transmits the emanations of its origin and our own. In doing this it
provides a cross-over between the seen and the unseen, between the
potential and the kinetic energies of that space we move in which is
not simply space: perhaps it is the soul of the universe; and perhaps
we are the organ of perception required by that soul.

The fancy offers itself that perhaps Portknockie has taken on this
power only since declining from its worldly success. Perhaps when
it was a thriving herring port this power was not in it; perhaps it had
first to lose the specialized power of what we recognize as useful
function before it could manifest the power of the potential, the
power of the one continuous rhythm of immanent change and
permutation that vibrates behind the appearances of things. Indif-
ferent to us it is, inhuman; yet to tune ourselves to it feels good, gives
us a sense of release from the hard bargain of the mortal contract.
Perceiving then the full nature of the power I abandon the fancy of
its accession; I know that this power of the potential has always
been in Portknockie. It was here when the nets were heavy with fish
and the brown sails prospered, but at that time when the harbour
was forested with the masts of Zulu boats and resounded with
strong shouts it would have been less apparent. Now the silent
empty harbour shows itself to us and requires our attention.

All round Portknockie harbour are great iron rings secured by
iron eyes to concrete and to stone, iron rings nearly as thick as my
wrist and with an aperture more than a foot across. Here I look at
one of them much older than the others, it lies flat on the concrete by
the inner harbour wall, thick flakes of brown rust on it like tree-
bark, the outer roundness of it rusted into flatnesses and angles like
a rough thick vine or a branch bent in a circle. The iron eye that
holds the ring is also like old wood, like a branch thrust up through
the concrete and doubling back into it. What does it say, this
iron-into-wood? It says what the ribs and columns of the crypt of
Canterbury Cathedral say: those stone columns are the trunks,
those stone ribs of the vaulting are the branches, they are the living
wood of Christ and year-king become trees of stone. They say what
this iron-become-wood says: Now I show it to you this way, now I
show it to you that way.

Near Gun Hill

ALAN BROWNJOHN

Once drawn to promontories where the sea
Is grey and intemperate, with sheer juts
Of rock into rapacious, upheaved waters . . .
At Hartland Point in fog a bursting roar
Blares out on time and space from the lighthouse
And deafens its own echoes; while inland
Merely a sweet haze drapes the sunset fields.
Or at Rhossili, or the Calf of Man:
A savagery interposes on the path
Of sun- or moonlight laid across that bleak
Table of restlessness, and breaks all thought.
Once drawn to this; and therefore not believing
Any disquiet on one rare windless day
Lying down and gazing on endless sands
On this eastern coast, line above line, and each
A deepening, dried yellow to the edge,
With the last line the horizon: all a stave
Still innocent of anything's notation
—And to feel suddenly how the huge chords
Don't dramatize themselves, don't flaunt themselves
In obvious frenzies here, but lie and wait
While the first creature of the swarm climbs slowly
Unsheathing a black wing and tilts one reed.

A Tide in the Affairs

RICHARD MABEY

I was nearly eighteen before I succeeded in getting as far north as the
Norfolk coast. One summer, a friend whose father had a converted
lifeboat moored at Blakeney offered to take some of us up in his
Land-Rover for a few days' holiday. There were, I think, ten of us in
the back, scrabbling about on top of each other like over-excited
puppies. I was the least travelled of the group, but for every one of
us East Anglia was an unknown country, an awkward pro-
tuberance (later we all came to call it the Ankle) out of mainstream
England. Was it an outback, a wilderness, or just a backwater, plain
and simple? The strange prospects that began to open out beyond
Newmarket only confused us further. American air bases floated
like mirages amongst the Breckland heaths, and we imagined we
could see the glint of their hateful missiles. The edges of the sandy
fields were lined with stunted pine windbreaks, unlike any hedges
we had ever seen; then, further on, there were no margins at all, and
the great washes of sugar-beet and barley broke abruptly against
the flint walls of medieval churches. Less than a hundred miles from
home we had stumbled on a landscape that to our inexperienced
eyes was cryptic and compelling, and we bounced about in the
Land-Rover in a thrill of expectation. When we swung into the long
straight reach of the Icknield Way just north of Brandon, Justin, our
driver and host, sensing our feeling of release but also his own new
responsibilities, hunched down towards the dashboard and began
changing into four-wheel drive with his foot.

We saw more kicking-out—a gesture which succeeded in being
nonchalant and supremely authoritative all at once—that evening
in the pub. Crow, whom we came to venerate as the local water-
spirit and who responded by making merciless sport with our
gullibility, had a trick with the bar-skittles. He would throw the
ball, aiming somewhere between the doorknob and the photograph
of the pre-war lifeboat crew that hung on the wall, and on the
backswing give it a flick of the foot that made it swoop round and
knock every skittle flat. Crow was in his late fifties then, the same
age as most of the men in the lifeboat crew in the photo. On the

rescue that the picture honoured the conditions had been so terrible that the men's hands had been frozen solid to the oars. Norfolk, that evening, began to look like a place where you could flex all manner of undiscovered muscles.

Yet even on those first visits the place sounded many old chords. It was the first time I had gone tribal since I was a child, when, with another gang, I had spent my holidays in the grounds of an abandoned mansion at the foot of our garden. We went out there first thing, built camps in trees and holes in the ground, churned milk on upturned bicycles, baked potatoes in wood fires, fought off invaders from the council estate on the far side of the park, and then went home for tea. We used it as our common, and always referred to it, rather imperiously, as 'The Field'. Everywhere else, just as airily, was 'Up The Top'. And up high, in ecstatic daydreaming on those hills to the south of our road, was where I spent most of the remainder of my youth. It was a patch of country that I clung to like a secret code, full of touchstones and private vistas that had to be visited in a precise and rigid sequence. It was right enough for a brooding adolescent I suppose, but when Norfolk arrived I was glad to be back with some company again, and with a landscape that seemed to have some of the perennial new-mintedness of those childhood mornings in The Field.

We spent that first Norfolk night, as we were to spend many more in the years to come, crammed into eccentric cavities of the old lifeboat (which was called, for reasons beyond any fathoming, *Dilemma X*). The lucky few had bunks. The rest of us found what spaces we could under tables and in the wheelhouse. In the morning I wriggled stiffly out of my own cranny near the bilges, found a porthole, and looked out on the sight that has kept me in thrall to this coastline ever since: a high tide swirling in over a mile of salt-marsh and lapping on the concrete quay where we were moored. There was not a single point of stillness. Terns hovered above the water and spikes of sea-lavender bent and bounced under the tide-race. Even the mud was alive, and slid out of the receding water with the moist shine of a new-born animal.

Our conventional views about landscape cannot cope with salt-marshes. They are neither sea nor dry land. They confound our notions of the timelessness of country places by never being the same in two successive hours. They can look, for a while, as comfortable and immemorial as old hay-meadows, yet twice a day they are fingered and reshaped by the sea. The men who go out on them to dig for lugworms work inland out of season, doing this and that on farms and gardens. They even talk of the mud-flats in terms of fields and ditches, yet they know that no tractor could ever drag them out if they were caught by tides that come in faster than a man can walk.

The local ferrymen we got to know showed their contempt for the shifting contours of the channel that linked Blakeney to the sea by bringing in their boats at the lowest possible water, holding the tiller with one hand and rolling a cigarette ('wibbling', they called it) with the other. We had no such confidence, and one journey up the spout in *Dilemma* per visit was quite enough. Nor did we venture out to the sea proper, but to the Pit, a natural haven sheltered by the long shingle spit known as Blakeney Point. The Point was always our goal. We could not get enough of it, and we struck out for it like the promised land even when *Dilemma* was immobile, and we had to wade out at low tide with black mud squirting between our toes. It was our Coral Island, an enchanted oasis of lagoons and shifting dunes, where seals basked and the air was full of the clamour of oyster-catchers and redshanks. Even when rain hung over the mainland this three-mile-long peninsula often lay under its own mysteriously clear strip of blue sky. The hollows between the dunes were sun-traps, and in summer it would have been easy to imagine ourselves in the South Seas. The tree-lupins smelt of coconut and the sea-pinks of honey. (Once, walking over marshes at Stiffkey on a blazing August day, I saw a true Norfolk mirage. The Point floated high above the horizon, stretched by the heat so that its dunes looked like the walls of a Moorish castle.)

When the tide went out it left little pools, just a few feet deep and warm enough not just to swim in but to doze in. Once we saw a great flock of terns swirling like ticker-tape above one of these pools and raining down upon a shoal of whitebait that had been stranded there. We never caught any fish ourselves, but we grubbed for cockles and cooked bundles of marsh samphire (wrapped in Bakofoil—we were no purists) over driftwood fires. We sometimes dreamed of spending whole days and nights out there, curled up under the dunes, but the fantasy of being castaways never gripped us strongly enough to do it. Our days on the Point were just a special kind of picnic, and in the evenings we wanted more ordinarily convivial pleasures. So when the tide was right we would row back to *Dilemma*, then to the flats on the landward side of the Pit and walk across a mile of glassy mud and rickety plank bridges to the pub at Morston. It was a hilarious, slithery journey even in the daylight, and how we used to make it back after closing time I do not know. Justin, never one to shirk his Captain's responsibilities, would not allow us to use torches in case we dropped them and fell away ourselves with night blindness (some of the creeks under those bridges were ten feet deep). So if there was no moon the only light was the phosphorescence that rippled about our feet as we splashed into the shallow water. Sometimes we could see our last footprints glowing for a brief instant in the damp sand behind us, as long-lived a trace as anyone leaves here. I learned much later that it was partly these marsh-lights that Justin thought had given the samphire that grew in these muds its name. Never having had a reason to see the word written he thought it was 'sand-fire'.

I have never understood those who talk of these marshes as desolate places. They can be remorselessly hard, particularly in winter, but they are never oppressive. They are too open for that. If you look east or west along the flats you can sometimes see for a dozen miles, up to the far side of the Wash if you are lucky. The view would swallow you if it were not for the rim of the sea itself. It is a shifting edge but it puts a comforting limit to things. Stand by it and look due north, and there is no land between you and the Arctic Circle. The North Sea here is as black as anywhere in Britain, and the locals—never at a loss for a telling epithet—call it the German Ocean. Yet turn round and look inland and you could be in the Cotswolds. In the mile or so that lies between the sea and the coast road, the marshes gradually pull themselves together. Nearest you are the bare sands, and the plastic, shifting muds; then the pastel wash of the first plants, the silver wormwood and lilac sea-lavender; then the claimed grazing land locked up behind the sea-walls; and finally, backed up against the low swell of the coastal hills, the little villages with their mighty churches, as compact and bright as if they were tucked in a real valley.

It is hard to feel really alone with a tide. It will come in, absolutely predictably, and always, eventually, recede. The signs spent water leaves on the sand and mud-flats are like a vanishing footprint—or,

Afon Gamlan, North Wales by John Blakemore

more, a handprint. The husbanding by the tides is what gives marshy landscapes their kinship with the infinitely more slowly moulded sceneries inland. It is as if a whole round of seasons—or a whole generation of farming—was enacted twice a day.

Every few years the sea breaks in more savagely, but even then the changes are transient. In the early months of 1976 a great storm breached sea-walls right along the coast and all the coastal habitats—beach, sand, mud-flat, salting—were thrown together in a mad jumble. The sea sprayed tongues of shingle far into the marsh, and hollowed out muddy pools in the middle of the beach. The rows of sea-blite bushes that grow along the margin between beach and mud were completely buried by shingle in many places. But by August that year their shoots had already started to reappear above the surface. I dug down below one of these new sprigs, down to the old and already decaying parent plants, and saw the new shoots, pallid but indomitable, pushing their way up through more than two feet of heavy pebbles.

Nothing can survive on the marshlands unless it is prepared to be adaptable. Once or twice every year, when the autumn/spring tides are boosted by north-easterly gales, the seaward edge of Blakeney floods. Most years the flood is treated as a kind of festival. Everyone gathers round the quay—a coastal community's village green—to see the tide in. The car-park attendant's booth usually bobs free and floats off amongst his charges, and as the water starts lapping the steps of the knitwear shop in the High Street, the more adventurous boat-owners go shopping in their tenders.

If you walk up this steep street at high tide you can get a measure of the sheer dominance of the water. It pushes the tide-line of spectators—cars, boats and all—before it, like flecks of spindrift. The street is so sheer that when the quay was used commercially the cargoes had to be edged down in carts harnessed to backward-walking horses. I once saw a less effectively braked bulldozer, clearing up flotsam after one of these flood tides, slide gracefully into the channel. When we tried to trundle a piano down the street the wheels became so hot they hissed in the puddles. Ancient landscapes have an imperative force that will never let you forget how and why they were formed.

The tribe has broken up now and gone its separate ways, and when I come back to this stretch of Norfolk I am usually by myself.

But the rhythms of the marsh landscape are as familiar company as they ever were. I still follow the old route up—past the airfields and squat pines, along the road from Fakenham that edges, maddeningly slowly, towards the coast. Then through the gorse and heather of Salthouse Heath, that lies on a ridge of sandy gravels that were dumped here by the last ice-sheet. You see the first glint of water; then, as you tip sharply down through the narrow strip of arable fields, the marsh suddenly fills the whole horizon, criss-crossed with silver dykes. You feel age and time falling away. Where you are standing was, five hundred years ago, the coastline. What you are looking at now is a sight that has never been seen exactly so before, nor ever will be again.

I drive as fast as I dare to Morston, kick off my shoes—that brazen gesture again—run out over the mud towards that thin blue line that hangs over the tide's edge, and wonder why I have ever left.

Landscape with Figures: Cornwall

ROBERT GITTINGS

> Patter of overheard talk,
> Shingle dashed against glass,
> Foam over inland fields,
> White blobs in blowing night,
> Dipping and floating in flocks
> Like moonmen landing on earth
> Under a herring-bone cloud
> With star trail threading between—
> Half memory and half dream,
> The singular timing of love,
> Extinct as the smoking, powdery
> Dust of a tufa cone,
> Yet red, returning, to flash
> Headland's revolving beam,
> Catching the pair that embrace,
> Transfixed, a landscape with figures.

Padstow

Sir John Betjeman

Some think of the farthest away places as Spitzbergen or Honolulu. But give me Padstow, though I can reach it any day from Waterloo without crossing the sea. For Padstow is in Cornwall and Cornwall is another country. And Padstow is farther away in spirit even than Land's End. It is less touristy than other fishing towns like Polperro and St. Ives: less dramatic than Boscastle or Tintagel: only just not a village, for it has more than two thousand inhabitants. It is an ancient unobvious place, hidden away from the south-west gales below a hill on the sandy estuary of the River Camel. It does not look at the open sea but across the tidal water to the sand-dunes of Rock and the famous St. Enodoc Golf Course. There is no beach, only an oily harbour and remarkably large prawns may be netted where the town drains pour into the Camel.

Green Southern Railway engines once came right into the brown and cream Great Western district of Cornwall, to reach Padstow. Launceston, Egloskerry, Otterham, Tresmeer, Camelford—and so on, down that windy single line. I know the stations by heart, the slate- and granite-built waiting rooms, the oil lamps and veronica bushes, the great Delabole Quarry, the little high-hedged fields, and I know where the smallholdings grow fewer and the fields larger and browner, so that I can see the distant outline of Brown Willy and Rough Tor on Bodmin Moor. Then the train goes fast downhill through high cuttings and a wooded valley. We round a bend and there is the flat marsh of the Camel, there are the little rows of blackish-green cottages along the river at Egloshayle and we are at Wadebridge, next stop Padstow. The next five and a half miles beside the broadening Camel to Padstow was the most beautiful train journey I knew. See it on a fine evening at high tide with golden light on the low hills, the heron-haunted mud coves flooded over, the sudden thunder as we cross the bridge over Little Petherick creek, the glimpses of slate roofs and a deserted jetty among spindly Cornish elms, the wide and unexpected sight of open sea at the river mouth, the huge spread-out waste of water with brown ploughed fields coming down to little cliffs where no waves break but only

70

salt tides ripple up and ebb away. Then the utter endness of the end of the line at Padstow—260 miles of it from London. The smell of fish and seaweed, the crying of gulls and the warm, moist, west-country air and valerian growing wild on slate walls.

The approach to Padstow I like most of all is the one I have made ever since I was a child. It is by ferry from the other side of the estuary. It was best in a bit of a sea with a stiff breeze against an incoming tide, puffs of white foam bursting up below the great head of distant Pentire and round the unapproachable cliffs of the rocky island of Newland which seems, from the ferry boat, to stand half-way between Pentire and Stepper Point at the mouth of the river. We would dip our hands in the water and pretend to feel seasick with each heave of the boat and then the town would spread out before us, its slate roofs climbing up the hillside from the wooden wharves of the harbour till they reached the old church tower and the semi-circle of wind-slashed elms which run as a dark belt right around the top of the town, as though to strap the town in more securely still against those south-west gales. Sometimes we would return on a fine, still evening, laden with the week's shopping, and see that familiar view lessen away from the ferry boat while the Padstow bells, always well rung, would pour their music across the water, reminding me of Parson Hawker's lines—

Come to thy God in time!
Thus saith their pealing chime
Youth, Manhood, Old Age past!
Come to thy God at last!

Padstow is a fishing port and a shopping centre. There is an ice factory, an attractive Georgian Customs House, a hideous post office, an electric-light company founded in 1911, and a gasworks founded in 1868, this last, beside sad and peeling Public Rooms of yellow stucco dated 1840.

Vast numbers of service people pour in today from a desert that has been made in the neighbouring parishes of St. Eval and St. Merryn—a form of desert known as an aerodrome.

But the chief fact about modern Padstow to interest fact-maniacs, starts with a mermaid. She was combing her hair and singing in the estuary, when a Padstow youth went walking along the cliff towards the open sea. He shot at her and in her rage she plunged down below the water and picked up a handful of sand which she threw towards Padstow, and that was the start of the Doom Bar. This bar is a bank of sand which for centuries has been slowly silting up the estuary.

In 1948 at a Town Council meeting a letter was read from a Yarmouth firm of ship owners: 'We have always been in the habit of sending our boats to Padstow, as we did last year, and we intend to do so again in 1949 during February, March, and April. Like everyone else, we are concerned about the silting up of the estuary, making it extremely difficult to manœuvre our ships in and out of port, and if action is not taken very soon we shall be unable to use the port at all, to our mutual detriment.' So there are hundreds of thousands of tons of agricultural silver sand, increasing and increasing. I can well remember how as a child I could see the hulks of ships which had been wrecked on the Doom Bar sticking up black out of the yellow sand. These are now all covered over. Who will take the sand away? And how will they do it? Miracles are always happening. In Padstow they are easier to believe in than in most places, because it is so ancient a town. So probably the port of Padstow will be saved, even if it is a Government Department that performs the miracle.

Slate-hung houses are built in a semi-circle round the harbour. Here and there the silver-blue tiled buildings are diversified by an old rose-coloured brick house and near me is a building called The Abbey House, with granite fifteenth-century quoins. A boy standing up in a dinghy propels her backwards across the calm, oily water by working an oar to and fro in the stern. I turn into the quiet square of the Ship Hotel and notice that Miss Tonkin's boot shop is no longer there, though her house with its ferns in the window and lace curtains, its lush, enclosed front and back gardens, still stands. I see that a jeweller's shop has been transformed into a souvenir haunt of tourists and new diamond-leaded panes look odd in the windows, and wooden beams, unknown in Cornwall, are fixed on to the outside walls. The main streets are, thank goodness, little altered. There's not much grand architecture in Padstow. It is all humble unobtrusive houses, three storeys high. Yet as soon as one of them is taken down, the look of the town suffers. I take one of the many narrow roads that lead up the hill. And as I reach the upper air near the church, I realize what a lot of gardens and houses there are in Padstow, though the place looks all slate from the waterside. For here one can look down at the roofs of the houses, on palms and ilex trees and bushes of hydrangeas peeping above slate walls. Narrow public passages pass right through houses under stone arches and lead past high garden walls, down steps under another house to a further street. And I begin to notice that this slate is not grey, as we are inclined to think is all Cornish slate, but a beautiful pale green, streaked here and there with reddish-brown. This is all hewn locally from the cliffs. Slate roofs grouted over with cement and then lime-washed, slate walls, slate paving stones and, as I near the churchyard gate, slate hedges as high as a house on either side of me, stuffed with ferns and pennywort. I saw the little purple flowers of ivy-leaved toadflax on these hedges blooming as late as November last. Above these stone hedges are holly bushes and beyond the holly the circling belt of Cornish elms. A wrought-iron gate opens into the churchyard. In tree-shaded grass are slate headstones with deep-cut lettering of the eighteenth and early nineteenth centuries and cherubs with ploughboy faces, Victorian marble stones to sailors with carved anchors and cables. The parish church of St. Petroc is built of a brown-grey slate and its large fifteenth-century windows are crisply carved out of that dark blue-black Cataclewse stone, a most beautiful hard stone for carving which lasts the centuries. The church is unusually large and lofty inside for a Cornish building. It was pleasantly restored in the last century. A huge monument with kneeling figures painted in reds and whites and yellows and blacks commemorates Sir Nicholas Prideaux, 1627, and leads me to Padstow's great house, Prideaux Place.

It stands on a grass clearing among elms, firs, and many ilex trees, that specially west-country tree, not far from the church, near the higher part of the town where late Georgian houses with ilex and palm-shaded gardens and glasshouses with geraniums and grapes in them, suggest the land agent, the doctor, retired tradesmen, and old sea captains. A sign saying 'No through road' encourages me to walk through, and I come to a low castellated slate wall in a toy-fort Gothic style, with a genuine Gothic door of dark-blue Cataclewse stone let into it. Behind this in full view of the road, is the E-shaped manor house. The eastern front looks over the road to its little-planted park and on to the distant low sand-hills across the estuary. The feathery slate walls are battlemented on top. Over the entrance porch, in the wings, and in the spaces between them, are noble

granite windows. Even the old lead rain-water heads are there, with
the Prideaux crest and initials on them. A large magnolia shelters in
one fold of the house and a Georgian semi-circular bay is just seen
on the south wing, looking across another part of the park. The
inside of the house is said to be full of panelling and wood carving
and plasterwork and fine furniture.

All this is Elizabethan and seventeenth century. And the church
and the houses in the town are medieval or Georgian. They seem
comparatively new. What becomes apparent about Padstow is that
it is even older than its oldest buildings. When the River Camel was
narrower and when woods waved in the estuary which are now
covered with sand, thirteen hundred years ago, St. Petroc, Servant
of God and son of a Welsh king, crossed the sea from Ireland in a
coracle and landed at Trebetherick on the other side of the water.
And then he crossed the river and founded a monastery which was
known as Petrocstow—that is to say Petroc's church—which we
now pronounce Padstow. Many miracles are recorded of him, tales
of his kindness to animals, his long prayers standing in a stream on
Bodmin Moor where to this day his little beehive cell, made of turf
and granite, survives. He raised the dead, cured the sick, tamed a
savage, serpent-eating monster. A medieval life of St. Petroc was
discovered recently which ended thus:

A woman, feeling thirsty one night, drank water out of a water-jug and
swallowed a small serpent [in consequence of which] she was for many
years in bad health. As no physicians benefited her, she was brought to the
holy man. He made a mixture of water and earth which he gave the sick
woman to drink, and immediately she had swallowed it she vomited a
serpent three feet long, but dead, and the same hour she recovered her
health and gave thanks to God.

After these and many such like miracles, Blessed Petroc, continually
longing for heavenly things, after afflicting his body with much rigour, full
of days departed to God, on the day before the nones of June. The sacred
body, therefore, worn out with fastings and vigils, is committed to the
dust, and the bosom of Abraham receives his spirit, the angels singing to
welcome it. At his tomb miracles frequently take place and his bones,
albeit dry, retain the power of his virtues. May his glorious merits inter-
cede for us with Christ, Who with the Father liveth and reigneth world
without end. AMEN.'

I do not know whether St. Petroc's day, the 4th of June, is still kept in Padstow church; it is in Bodmin parish church and in most of the other thirty or forty churches in Wales, Devon, and Cornwall which are dedicated to him. His cult has survived too in Brittany and at Loperec (Locus Petroci) they have a statue of him, a more lively one than the little stone one in Padstow church. It shows a benign, bearded man in a spangled cloak, in one hand he holds the gospels and with the other he strokes a thin, nobbly little deer which has jumped up to him and put its forepaws on his breast. Blessed St. Petroc! He was the chief of all Cornish saints, a man of pervading gentleness.

St. Petroc may be neglected in Padstow today. But the Hobby-horse is not. Whether it came in with the Danes who sacked the town in 981 and drove St. Petroc's monks to Bodmin or whether it was a pagan rite which St. Petroc himself may have witnessed with displeasure, I leave to antiquarians to dispute. The Padstow Hobby-horse is a folk revival which is almost certainly of pagan origin. Moreover, it is as genuine and unselfconscious as the Morris Dancing at Bampton-in-the-Bush, Oxfordshire, and not even broadcasting it or an influx of tourists will take the strange and secret character from the ceremonies connected with it. For this is what happens. On the day before May Day, green boughs are put up against the houses. And that night every man and woman in Padstow is awake with excitement. I knew someone who was next to a Padstow man in the trenches in the 1914 War. On the night before May Day, the Padstow man became so excited he couldn't keep still. The old 'obby 'oss was mounting in his blood and his mates had to hold him back from jumping over the top and dancing about in no-man's-land.

Now imagine a still night, the last of April, the first of May. Starlight above the chimney-pots. Moon on the harbour. Moonlight shadows of houses on opposite slate walls. At about two in the morning the song begins. Here are the words.

> With a merry ring and with the joyful spring,
>> For summer is a-come unto day
> How happy are those little birds which so merrily do sing
>> In the merry morning of May.

Then the men go round to the big houses of the town singing below the windows a variety of verses—

76

Padstow

'Arise up Mr Brabyn I know you well afine
You have a shilling in your purse and I wish it were in mine.'

And then on to a house where a young girl lives—

'Arise up Miss Lobb all in your smock of silk
And all your body under as white as any milk.'

Morning light shines on the water and the green-grey houses. Out
on the quay comes the Hobby-horse—it used to be taken for a drink
to a pool a mile away from the town. It is a man in a weird mask,
painted red and black and white, and he wears a huge hooped skirt
made of black tarpaulin which he is meant to lift up, rushing at the
ladies to put it over one of their heads. The skirt used to have soot in
it. A man dances with the Hobby-horse carrying a club. Suddenly,
at about 11.30 in the morning, there is a pause. The Hobby-horse
bows down to the ground. The attendant lays his club on its head
and the day song begins, a dirge-like strain.

'Oh where is St. George? Oh where is he, O?
He's down in his long boat. All on the salt sea, O.'

Then up jumps the Hobby-horse, loud shriek the girls, louder sings
the crowd and wilder grows the dance—

With a merry ring and with a joyful spring
For summer is a-come unto day
How happy are those little birds which so merrily do sing
In the merry morning of May.

Herne Bay

NINA BAWDEN

Places we have known in childhood exert a peculiar spell of enchantment. Returning in later life, we can sometimes still see what we once saw. Like the wrinkles that have mysteriously appeared on our faces, the jungles of concrete and brick, the roads and retirement bungalows, are only *temporary*; the youthful skin, the green fields, are still there beneath.

Nine years old, a ghost from my own past, I sit beside my tall aunt in the little train that rattles the long length of the pier, and complain of the cold. 'There is no land between Herne Bay and the North Pole. That', says my aunt, 'is why the air is so exceptionally healthy.' This information fills me with a fierce, romantic excitement. Peering through the penny telescope across the heaving waters of the Thames estuary I see, not passing steamers, but ice-floes. Once (I am quite sure of it) I saw a whale.

The telescope is on the sea front, near the photographer's kiosk. Beside the kiosk is an ancient, stuffed bear on which I sit to have my picture taken. If I put my finger into the hole on the back of his neck I can pull out small lumps of his stuffing—as distinctive a sensual pleasure as the first gritty bite at a tacky ball of candy-floss, and the slap-and-suck of blue mud round my bare foot at low tide.

Lines of striped deck-chairs flap on the promenade, and on the roof of the bandstand, brave flags crack and stream in the cold wind from the Pole. Like the clock tower and the handsomely decorated public lavatories, the bandstand was built, my aunt tells me, at a time when it was hoped that Herne Bay would become a rival to Brighton. 'Common' people, she explains, go to sandy Margate. Herne Bay's shingle beaches attract 'a better class of visitor'. This is why the fun-fair (which I am only allowed to visit once every holiday) is tucked away at the shabbier end of the town, along with the 'trippery' shops that sell rude postcards and rock and false teeth made of sugar.

The bear has gone now, the little train was a war casualty, and all that remained of the beautiful pier, when I last saw it, was a broken, fragile finger, stretching out to sea. But even when I was nine, it must have been clear that the Brighton dream was a lost cause. There were no grand hotels, and once away from the pier and the bandstand and the fine row of mock-Regency houses that faced it, the promenade came to an end rather abruptly, as if the builders had unexpectedly run out of materials, or money, or had simply lost heart. Defeated by changing times, perhaps—once people could come for the day in their motor cars, boarding-houses stood empty. Or perhaps by a deadlier enemy: the hungry North Sea.

At one end of the town the Downs rose, seeming to tilt upwards in preparation for battle. On the top, on the cropped grass, children flew kites and old people walked dogs. There was a splendid view of the pier and of a bubbling yellow line far out at sea that my aunt said was sewage. From the highest point a wooden stairway, the 'Hundred Steps', descended to a long, empty beach where the sea hissed on pebbles as if a giant broom swept, rhythmically, huge piles of broken glass. The bare brown cliffs reared above this bleak shore, hollowed out by the sea, capped with a narrow frill of grass on the sinister overhang like green icing on a chocolate cake. These cliffs were treacherous; slabs of soft clay could collapse without warning. Houses that one summer were safely inland were teetering on the edge by the next. One winter an entire garden was neatly lopped from its bungalow and fell two hundred feet. From the top we could see it; rose bushes still flowering; an ornamental pond still intact, a red garden gnome still fishing beside it.

I am grown up by this time, but although I hold my children back from the cliff edge with a mother's anxiety, I am as excited as they are. Herne Bay belongs to my childhood and I still see it with a child's eye; with that curious lens that sometimes opens up in the mind, letting in light and memory.

We go to the far end of the Bay where the sea slips in over the mud-flats, and reedy dykes criss-cross the land like a chess-board. Between the dykes, cattle are grazing. My aunt (the same aunt, my tall aunt grown older) says that this part of the coast is called The Land of the King's Cows. And, at once, the lens opens. The cows (I can see now) are Royal Beasts. The sky is blue, the sun hot; on the other side of the water the Isle of Sheppey trembles in a distant heat haze like a sleeping, grey dragon. I am walking on grass, beside the long, curving, sea-wall, but I know—my *feet* know—what the broken white shells of the foreshore will feel like when I jump down

upon them. I lift my face to the wind and breathe in the smell of the
estuary which since the tide is low is a mud smell, stinking ooze,
drying seaweed, not very agreeable, but to me at this moment, it is
the smell of childhood and innocence. I am nine years old and
taking the first, salty breath of my holiday; my first gulp of what
was prescribed as healthy ozone, Herne Bay's 'exceptional' air.

Aldeburgh: the Vision and the Reality

SUSAN HILL

There are two Aldeburghs, and yet they are one. Yet not one.
Separate and distinct. The first may belong to anyone; certainly to
those who live there, and to its visitors, festival and fishing people
and families on holiday, to all who enjoy it for a day or for years,
who work and play there. I lived and worked there for spells, made
friends, felt both at home and not so, and now, occasionally, and
less often than I would like, I go back. I was not born there, I do not
belong to the county of Suffolk at all, but much farther up the same
coast, in Yorkshire. My ties with Aldeburgh are all of a different
order. Yes, there is that real small town, what is left of it after
hundreds of years of storm and tide have washed into it and it has
crumbled and fallen, so that the Moot Hall is at the very edge, where
once it was in the very centre. There is that visible, visitable place;
from Liverpool Street to Saxmundham and then take to the road,
and there are fast dual carriageways, now, converging upon it from
three directions, and the sea at the other door. There are people who
live in houses painted fondant Suffolk pink and cream and grey, or
else in terraces cut into the hill like tiers of a cake; people who shop
for bread and gloves and aspirin, in and out of the long, surprisingly
broad High Street, where small shopkeepers still flourish, for this
is one of the last places which does not look like every other
place.

   This is the real town, yes, with the church at the top of the hill and
the sea at the bottom and lanes like fingers of a spread hand poking

out to reach it here and here and here, so that you only need to follow any one of them along, to fetch out before and beside its great greyness, only need to follow the salt wind in your nostrils and the hiss and boom and suck of it in your ears.

It is a place much favoured by the energetic retired and for holidays by the intellectual middle classes and a place of boats, pleasure boats, leisure boats, and the working fishing boats, dragged up on to the shingle. It is the music town, with a Festival every year since 1948, well known the world over and in summer, thronged with drummers and pluckers, bowers and blowers, a busy town of golf and whist, Red Cross and Royal National Lifeboat Institution.

Yes, all that, and it is indeed real enough and very pleasing.

But for me, there is another Aldeburgh, and perhaps it is not real. It is as though I open a door in my mind, a door that leads into my own past and to parts of my inner self, a place of my own imagination, which I have written about under different guises in different books, and I am still haunted by it, dream of it.

It was Britten, of course, who brought me to Aldeburgh, he was the Pied Piper and I followed his music until I came to it and heard it, at the heart, on the moan of the wind and in the cries of the curlews, in the thunder of the sea, and the stillness of it, too, as the moonlight lay over it on quiet, clear nights. The beach, the marshes, and the names of all the places around and about, and in, and in between, was like a country invented by his genius.

I find it impossible to be detached about Aldeburgh. I could not write of it plainly and baldly for any guide book, as 'short history, principal buildings, climate, special attractions'. For not only did I first come to it already brimming over with emotion about it, a sense of the place and a passion for it ready formed, not only was it even then partly unreal. I also spent much time in it at a particularly crucial highly charged and rare time of my life, so that I know Aldeburgh through my own emotions and my creative imagination, and through each book that I wrote there and which has left its mark upon me. It is the place in which I experienced deep joy and fulfilment and satisfaction, where I worked best of all and most easily and felt free as a bird. I make it sound romantic and unique and significant and so, for me, it was.

The Kingdom of the Shore

Every year I rented a house there from the depths of winter into very early spring, overlooking—almost *in*—the sea. I saw frost on the shingle and it was sometimes so cold I felt I had lost a skin, the wind battered at walls and windows. And there were those beautiful, vibrant days of late February and March, cloudless, cold, which had a piercing clarity in the air, and there seemed to be sky everywhere, pale sky and silver sea, with the land and houses merely a streak between. Larks spiralled up, the sun shone on the river at Slaughden as on a sheet of metal, the reeds and rushes rattled and shook, dry, dry. On such days, I walked inland for miles and saw no one, I made up page after page in my head, absorbed, concentrated, taut, yet seeing things too, waders in the mud, a heron, still as a tree-stump, the individual blades of grass. There was such a spirit in the air of that place, felt, heard, sensed, glimpsed, in the water and the sky and in the cries of birds.

I wrote all morning, looking up to see a fishing boat or the trawlers that sailed slowly in the far distance, and always the sea, moving about within itself, ruminative, grey, blue, violet, silver, it sang in my ears all day, all night.

I tramped the shingle, too, a noisy walk, head down into the screaming wind, and the gulls shrieked and reeled crazily about, and at night, I was sometimes afraid, and pulled the cat up on to my lap for comfort. For I was always alone there, and alone inside myself, too, that kind of life and work is necessarily utterly lonely. I would not have had it otherwise, and alone, you see and know what is hidden and blurred to you in company, you live on a different level, sensations, ideas, truths, the ghosts of the place, rise up and crowd your consciousness. I could never have been as I was, or written just what I did, in any other place in the world.

Then, sometimes, I would open the window wide on early March mornings, and sit with the sun full on my face and laugh to myself, it was so lovely, and then go out for fish, fresh caught, and dip my toes in the icy sea, and run, run over the stones, or throw them, ducks and drakes, or simply stand, watching some ship break the line of the horizon.

I knew, also, extreme, shattering grief there and the experience, the memory of it, are bound up with my view of the town, too. I remember how I stood and stared, stared down at the sea lapping over one patch of shingle, and could neither believe nor understand the appalling thing that had happened. That day changed my view of the place forever.

Then, I stopped going there to live alone and work. I have visited since, for days and weekends, but when at leisure and accompanied and so it has been the real, outward, everyday Aldeburgh that I have come to, and my presence there has been somehow superficial. Yet the other town is still there. It must be. I would only have to turn a corner and stand alone in wind and rain, to listen, remember.

For the one place I feel warm affection, and friendship, I enjoy it, recommend it, look it up in guide books and history books, I should like my family to remember it as the unspoilt town for happy seaside holidays.

And the other place. . . . Ah, that Aldeburgh I hold within me, set as in the amber you may find on the beach there, it is a landscape of the spirit.

RELICS
AND LOCATIONS

We picnic by these graves, these strata of the dead . . .

JOHN MATTHIAS, *Epilogue from a New Home*

Nottingham Castle

ALAN SILLITOE

Clouds love floodwater: play with
Distorted shekels among fresh grass
Seen from the Castle Top:
Binoculars ring the distance like a gun.
The ageing heart constricts
A twist of paper
With life's writing packed
In a script of tunic-red.
A parchment one year less than fifty old
Constructs a shield of seven-times-seven.

Serrated roofscape left and right
In shining slate; churches lurch
And chimneys lift; towers and modern
Blocks block visions. The 'Robin Hoods'
Paraded on this scoured parapet,
And practised azimuths of far-off points,
Eyes watering at southern hills
A half-day's march away:
'They'd have to swim the bloody Trent,
God-damn their goldfish eyes!'

Musket balls rush, break glass,
Make rammel: the mob
Did more damage than a foreign army,
Set rafters sparking, and painted
Pillars with the soot of anarchy.
Nottingham Lambs came up through
Lanes and twitchels, while the Trent
(Turbulent and sly) inky-rippling
The scarlet night, was no one's enemy,
Not even to douse the fires out.

The Council got it—finally:
A fine museum stonily protected
By Captain Albert Ball V.C.
Who thrust into a cloud-heap above Loos
Hoping for his forty-second 'kill',
But ended as a concrete man (with
An angel overlooking him) on the lawn
Of Nottingham's squat fort,
Guarding tunnels in the rock by which
Young Mortimer stalked to his Queen of Death.

Memory stands behind me
On that terrace and (like many suicides)
Thinks to take a flying leap into
A never-waking sleep. Forty years ago
I reached bemused for that same view,
But no big push came hard enough.
Only a good long gaze was needed:
Sailing barges drifted on the Leen
(Before my time) took me with them,
A whole fleet tunnelling my love.

I leave a ghost near that black wall,
Mesmerized at never having fallen;
Clocks toll off dark boxes of the night,
Every quarter-hour maddeningly
Dropped and buried in the dark,
A dream-life stifled beyond reach.
My footprints live, and eyes,
And hills that sleep dive with me,
To more clock hammers
Flattening minutes that won't talk again.

Following close, the rest is pain,
Another brain shot down in sleep.
Rich Master Robin Hood robs me
Who am not so rich of time,
And gives it to the poor who have enough.

Nottingham Castle
The whimsical robber stands outside the walls
While Death with its sonic boom
Smashes sunlight through the horizon's window
Back into the clock at dawn.

Bosworth Field

Geoffrey Moorhouse

The inscription on the boulder says that 'Richard, the last Plantagenet King of England, was slain here 22nd August 1485', and it
means that our history took one of its more decisive turns at this
spot five centuries ago. In this small paddock where the boulder
stands, the Tudors gained the monarchy at a stroke and a remarkable period for the English was begun. Before that century was out,
John Cabot had sailed west from Bristol to discover the New-
found-land, and the first seed of an empire had been sown. Within
another hundred years, the world resounded to the achievements of
the Elizabethan age—and we take great comfort from that memory
in our own less distinguished times. History may or may not have
dealt harshly with the character of Richard III, but there is no
getting away from the fact that from the moment Henry Tudor's
victory on the battlefield of Bosworth made him King Henry VII,
the national fortunes were much improved.

The Wars of the Roses, I was given to understand very early in
life, had a particular significance for a good Lancashire lad such as
myself, though the only battlefields mentioned in family reminis-
cence were those of Old Trafford, Headingley, and Bramall Lane. I
remember my astonishment when I reached my Pennine grammar
school and discovered that the most crucial encounter had, in fact,
taken place in the middle of Leicestershire, and that the historical
connection with the two northern counties was by no means as
close as I had been led to suppose. True, the city of York mourned
Richard deeply when he was killed, and his standard that day on
Bosworth Field had included a representation of the white

rose—but one dominated by a much larger image of the white boar. Henry's banner had flaunted a dragon, and the red rose was nobody's symbol until some time after the Houses of Lancaster and York had come to terms under the new king. Henry, indeed, was the son of a Welsh country gentleman, and until marching to fight Richard in the Midlands he had spent much of his young life in France. If it comes to that, Richard himself had a certain amount of French blood (as well as a drop of distant Spanish) waiting to be spilled that day. It was, I think, the untidiness of allegiances then which, casting oblique doubts on the provenance of my own neat pedigree, discouraged me from going forth to inspect Bosworth Field for many, many years. Besides, I have never had much taste for military history, and such English battlefields as I have chanced upon have done little to increase it: you are usually lucky to find a monument marking the area, with not another aid in sight. But Leicestershire County Council have made the site of Henry Tudor's victory a model of what such things should be. Without in any way defiling the landscape, they have provided abundant information with a degree of imagination that, generally speaking, the Americans bring to bear on their past much more than we do on ours. Exhibitions and films are to be found in a converted farmhouse: better still, you can walk where the soldiers fought, and at every vantage point unobtrusive signs indicate precisely what happened over the ground you see.

It is, of course, misleading to think of the site as a 'field' in the modern sense. Those two medieval armies were deployed over several square miles of the countryside if you include the position most cunningly chosen by Lord Thomas Stanley for his 4,000 troops when preparations for the battle began. He had brought them down from Cheshire in answer to King Richard's call and, before dawn on that Monday, he had arranged them some distance away from the chief combatants, so that they could be thrown into the conflict on behalf of whichever side appeared to be winning. When day broke, some 12,000 men were marshalled around Richard's standard on Ambion Hill, with the sun rising at their backs. Facing them at the bottom of the western slope was Henry Tudor with an army half the size. Watching thoughtfully across rolling ground to the north was Stanley's contingent, maybe knowing as well as their leader that they were not the only troops on

Spittal of Glenshee, Perthshire by Chris Jennings

whom Richard would be unwise to rely. His 12,000 included men commanded by the Earl of Northumberland, who was so half-hearted in support of the king that he never took part in the battle at all. The starting odds against Henry were not nearly as high as the bare figures suggest.

If you stand on Ambion Hill today your view is of rural England at its unspectacular but lovely norm. This is gently curving country-side (the hill itself is less than 400 feet above the sea), which glows in summer with much ripening corn, is crossed haphazardly by hawthorn hedges, and is as comforting as a parkland with trees. The remarkable thing is not how much but how little it will have changed since the last battle of the Roses was fought. Some miles away, the spire of St. Peter's Church in Market Bosworth pokes above the dark outline of a wood, and that is exactly what Richard would have seen that morning if he had looked beyond the pre-varicating Stanley and his men. Many of the oaks now rising out of cornfields were also growing then, and other trees have regenerated where fifteenth-century trunks stood. Progress has been very kind in its small alterations to this land. The two or three B-roads that potter between some of the high hedges are invisible from here. So is the Ashby canal, which eighteenth-century navvies cut around the contours of the undulating ground. As for the railway, that has been and gone, leaving a grassy furrow to be overgrown by rose-bay, willow-herb, and briar. The biggest change of all has been the disappearance of the marsh that swept round the bottom of Ambion on Richard's left flank, and on Henry's right. A plantation has been standing there these many years now, giving much cover for pigeons when the farmers go after them with guns.

There were guns at Bosworth Field, though artillery was then an infant craft. Warfare had not advanced by much from its experi-ences at Crécy and Agincourt, where archers turned the course of battles almost without help, where knights and men-at-arms dis-mounted and fought hand to hand beside the bows. But the infantry and horsemen here in 1485 were augmented by gunners who could fire four-pound cannon balls a thousand yards. It was they who took the first turn once the ritual manœuvring of the armies—a part of chivalry as much as of tactics—was done. Under the rising sun, Richard's four-pounders opened fire down Ambion Hill, their target easily within range. Then his bowmen dashed forward a little and loosed off a volley of their own at Henry's ranks. After them came a mass of men on horse and on foot, pouring downhill in a headlong charge. The slope of Ambion is not a steep one, and anyone looking up it from the Tudor front lines would have seen little but an engulfing wave of armour and weapons bearing down. It would have needed much courage to stand fast and fire arrows in return as that wave approached; but that is what Tudor's troops did. Even before the armies clashed the carnage would have been terrible towards the bottom of that hill, where grain now sways in the August breeze with the sound of receding surf. When the two sides merged, it was men hacking at each other with sword and pike, halberd and axe, in the ultimate, the most sickening horror of war. Still Henry's men did not break, though it could only be a matter of time before the greater numbers of Plantagenet's troops wore them down.

At a safe distance behind his soldiers, Henry Tudor sought salvation in that phalanx of arms still standing watchfully away to the north. With an escort he began to ride towards Stanley's position, to ask for the lord of Cheshire's commitment to his side. From his own security on top of Ambion Hill, Richard saw Henry move off, and guessed what was likely to happen next. Then he did the one thing that could instantly win the day for his crown, in an age which ordained that if a leader killed his adversary the battle was over and done. With his shield over his chest and his lance levelled ahead, the king spurred his white horse into a tearing gallop down the hill towards Henry and his bodyguard. That dash, with a handful of horsemen galloping with him, has been described as 'the last real charge of its kind, the swan-song of medieval English chivalry'. Its force was such that Richard's lance impaled Henry's standard-bearer, William Brandon, and it was all sword work after that, as the king frantically tried to get at his challenger. At that moment Stanley at last made his move, and his 4,000 men were flung on to Richard's flank, with Lord Thomas's younger brother, Sir William Stanley, in the lead.

It is possible that the king was knocked off his horse by the sheer weight of cavalry crashing into that group of struggling men. Or maybe, as some have thought, Richard's charger became bogged down in the marshy ground below Ambion Hill and he was forced to dismount. Perhaps, as Shakespeare imagined, he did cry 'A horse!

95

A horse! My kingdom for a horse!' I have no doubt that his end was as appalling as Olivier portrayed it when he made the film of Shakespeare's play: a man on foot, then writhing on the earth, while swords slashed and chopped at his head, his trunk, his limbs. For that, Henry Tudor had marched on Bosworth Field, and with that he became King Henry VII of England. In one of the hawthorn bushes that still abound nearby, a soldier named Reginald Bray found Richard's gold diadem, which had fallen from his helmet in the fight. It was placed on Henry's head when he was acclaimed in the village of Stoke Golding after the battle was over. A new dynasty had taken the English throne in little more than an hour's bloody work. Bosworth Field was finished before breakfast time had come.

Where Richard fell, that inscribed boulder has been put on a stone base below a high embankment of the canal. A slip of a stream gurgles along its ditch at one end of the paddock and, at the other, cows peer and ruminate over the hedge. An occasional vehicle hums down the lane, which is thickly dunged from the daily passage of cattle between pasture and farm. It is utterly peaceful here now, as it was before that battle was fought with all its gallantry and brutality, with all its violence and treachery. Healing is in the air of this place, for men have been careful with it since. But the only glow I have felt on contemplating the battle itself has been from words written by a Spanish friar the year after Bosworth Field was done.

Three hundred soldiers who fought on Henry's side joined the last European Crusade, to take Granada from the Moors in 1486. This Friar Antonio Agapida observed them closely there,

men who had been hardened in certain civil wars which had raged in their country. They were a comely race of men, but too fair and fresh for [the appearance of] warriors. They were huge feeders, also, and deep carousers; and could not accommodate themselves to the sober diet of our troops, but must fain eat and drink after the manner of their own country. They were often noisy and unruly, also, in their wassail; and their quarter of the camp was prone to be a scene of loud revel and sudden brawl. They were withal of great pride; yet it was not like our inflammable Spanish pride . . . their pride was silent and contumelious. Though from a remote and somewhat barbarous island, they yet believed themselves the most perfect men upon earth. . . . With all this, it must be said of them, that they were marvellous good men in the field, dexterous archers, and powerful with the battle-axe. In their great pride and self-will, they always sought to

96

press in their advantage, and take the post of danger. . . . They did not rush forward fiercely, or make a brilliant onset, like the Moorish and Spanish troops, but went into the fight deliberately and persisted obstinately, and were slow to find out when they were beaten.

X = ?

GLYN JONES

I am loth to reveal the name or the exact location of the place I am concerned with and shall either not do so at all or delay supplying the information until the last possible moment. The reasons for my reluctance will emerge later but please in the meantime allow me for as long as is practicable to refer to it simply as X.

I am at the seaside, deep in the rural Wales of farms, fields, cottages, hedges, woods, and villages, and also of history, and memory, and myth, almost as palpable as these. The sands I am standing on are not strictly sea-sands, although being extensive, firm, and golden they have every appearance of being so. The village of X is situated on the estuary of a Welsh river, broad and splendidly open to the sea, and what come washing over these beaches when the seas flood in are the tidal waters of Carmarthen Bay. Opposite me, on the river's further bank, as much as a mile away, stretch out the white houses of a pretty village, behind which stands Iscoed, the isolated and rather boring mansion that was the home of Sir Thomas Picton, a Welsh general killed at Waterloo. A much more remarkable man than Picton lived later in that village itself, in a house called Cobden Villa. This was Hugh Williams, described as 'solicitor and political agitator'. (Richard Cobden the English statesman was his brother-in-law.) Williams as a young man married a woman twenty-five years older than he was. She lived to be ninety and a couple of months after her death he married a young woman thirty-nine years his junior by whom he had four sons. But it was not the rather bizarre pattern of Williams's marital career that made him prominent and memorable, it was his passionate involvement with the radical politics of Chartism, and with the

Rebecca Riots. These last were organized attacks on the toll-gates that infested the turnpike roads of West Wales in the first half of the last century, to the mounting fury of the farmers who had to pay each time they drove their carts through them. Groups of young countrymen, many mounted and dressed as women (someone had found a passage in the Book of Genesis about the daughters of Rebecca destroying the gates of their enemies) materialized unpredictably at night near some toll-house, burnt the gates and then melted away into the darkness. There was a great to-do, people got killed, others were deported and the dragoons had to be brought in to restore order. Williams achieved considerable fame, or notoriety, in his capacity of radical solicitor, since he was prominent in the defence of those rioters unlucky enough to get caught. It is of interest that his grandson and namesake served the West End stage well earlier in this century both as playwright and actor and another descendant frequently graces our television screens with his handsome presence.

But our concern is really with X, and only marginally with her picturesque partner seen over the water, with the colourful yachts and the attractive houses. Let me again take up my stance on the beach of X and turn my back on the waters of the estuary. Far on my right the lovely cliff-girt sands peter out in marshland where a baffled stream distributes itself on its way to the river, and where the great black ribs of the old wrecked sailing boats, the *Falcon*, the *Sarah*, the *Primrose*, in my childhood rotted on the mud. Somewhere a little further up the river, perhaps another mile or two beyond the marsh, what must have been a rather splendid cavalcade crossed over the water in 1188 from shore to shore. This was the retinue of Baldwin, Archbishop of Canterbury, making a circular tour of Wales to preach the Third Crusade, and with him was the Lord Rhys, a Welsh prince, one of the richest and most powerful of the medieval potentates. We know about all this because another of the party was Gerald the Welshman, Giraldus Cambrensis, Gerald de Barri, a Norman-Welsh aristocrat who wrote a brilliantly journalistic account of the whole jamboree. Gerald came of a remarkable family. He had a granny whose marital adventures were even more egregious than those of Hugh Williams. She was beautiful Nest, mistress of Henry I, known as the Helen of Wales because, the daughter of one Welsh prince, she was abducted by another from her Norman husband's castle about thirty miles north-west of X. Poor brilliant, charming Gerald, more than anything he wanted to be Bishop of St. David's but, poor dab, he never was.

Far on my left, at the other end of the sands, more than a mile from the green marsh, rises the massive headland of Parc yr Arglwydd, the Lord's Park, a great green cap of pasture fitted on to a jut of vertical black cliffs. Having been brought up back in biblical times, so to speak, I associated in my childhood the Lord involved with the one I heard about in chapel; I still do not know which of the many individuals who have been granted the Lordship of X is intended by the title—the Normans de Clare or de Burley? the Lord Rhys before mentioned? Margaret of Anjou, Queen of England? the Dukes of Bedford, Buckingham, or Cornwall? or one of the Welsh peers? If it is true, as an Irish poet has it, that a landscape, a hill, a field, a cliff, a bay, becomes the property of the one who, absent, yearns for it, and, present, in love possesses it, then I myself, a landless man, am a considerable proprietor within the confines of X. Anyway, the map name for that headland at the beach's seaward end is Wharley Point and beyond it for me in childhood, even in the sunniest weather, lay only darkness and the menacing uproar of the vast gulleries there and the dread of *terra incognita*. Not so a famous poet I knew in the Thirties. For him that sinister and raucous wilderness held no terrors—but the bit about him can wait.

Right before me now, above the cliffs, towering majestically on the great eminence of its green hill, stands the castle of X, dominating beach, river-mouth, and the village hidden from sight behind its hill; a beautiful and noble ruin which still retains the lineaments of awe and majesty imparted to it by its early possessors—Gilbert de Clare, Maredudd ap Gruffyd, William de Chamville, the Lord Rhys and so on. Its ancient history, like that of many such imposing and picturesque structures, is one of unrelenting greed, violence and barbarity and its noblest moments for me are now, when, delivered from the slaughterhouse of the past, it stands majestic and useless in the full glare of the afternoon sun, looking down upon groups of children bathing on the beach or picnicking among the rocks of the cliff; or when its beauty was being captured by the brush of Turner; or when a local farmer used its courtyard as an additional meadow for his cows. From its high towers those with sufficiently muscular hams will be able to see behind the castle in summer weather the whole field-patterned sweep of the Welsh countryside, the unutterable tranquillity of rural Wales; and before him, down there below the cliffs, the broad estuary, and the vast sheet of the open sea beyond, blue and shining and smooth as solid tin, and resting upon its polish in the far distance the Gower peninsula, terminating in the grey sea-dragon of Worm's Head.

So far I have said little about the village of X itself. It is in two distinct parts. To my right, beyond the cliff but slightly higher than the beach, and separated from it by a width of grass, in summer a mass of buttercups, extends a long row of very pleasant houses, infinitely varied in size and design, some with gardens before them, called the Green. No English village green surely was ever like this in shape or situation. Behind it and parallel with it, higher up the low hill, is the village itself, a long, gently sloping main street with houses on both sides leading to the square—more triangle really—with its shops and pubs and its ancient church, now dedicated to St. Stephen, and referred to in records as early as 1170. Dotted around the village, never far from the main street, are three chapels, a junior school, a nice hotel (once one of the local big houses), and the homes of a Welsh literary figure, of an American poet (a part-time resident), and of a fine artist-craftsman in glass and metal. In conspicuous isolation on the hill between the end of the village street and the castle's eminence stands the Plas, its imposing façade white, pillared, and porticoed. This is the ancient big house of the parish, the home for generations of the local landowners. Its most notable occupant however was not a member of the Carmarthen squirearchy; it was Sir John Williams, Bart., court physician to Queen Victoria and a dedicated and generous bibliophile who collected books, manuscripts and prints of Welsh and Celtic interest. He transferred and bequeathed his ultimately vast library, together with considerable sums of money, to Wales, in order that a great library might be established here. His dream was realized when the National Library of Wales, of which he was the virtual founder, was established in Aberystwyth in 1909. This he lived to see.

Those who remember Dylan Thomas's story *A Visit to Grandpa's* will recall the dotty old gentleman driving up the main street of the village and stopping the governess cart, 'pulled by a short, weak pony', outside the Edwinsford Arms. That pub is at present a private house and the 'Sticks' that Dylan refers to later in his story are now much diminished in acreage and charm. These Sticks were in fact a grove of noble straight-trunked trees, mostly towering beeches, grouped on top of the cliffs below the castle; and here, earlier in this century, the visitors to X elected annually the mock Mayor of the village. A wooden railed platform stood in the middle of the wood's clearing. The audience sat on benches arranged in semi-circles around it and on seats fixed from tree-trunk to tree-trunk, listening to the hilarious fantasies of the candidates for mayoral honours, one promising in his election speech an almighty umbrella which would be opened to cover the entire village and its environs when the rain came to spoil the holidays. Another explained his proposed system of ducts from Pantglas, a local dairy farm, which would pipe the milk direct from the cows to the thirsty visitors waiting in the village square below; another was dedicated to the construction of a splendid rainbow bridge across the river estuary to avoid the crossing by ferryboat from the other side, which sometimes could be a stormy passage. In the Sticks too, in the gentle sunlight falling green through the glass lace of the leaf-fringed beeches, were held the visitors' amateur concerts and *eisteddfodau*, singer after singer going up on to the platform, and reciters, and public speakers, and debaters, and comedians, all cheerfully to compete for local *gloire* and a pittance of a prize. But the churchyard gate the old gentleman looked over in *A Visit to Grandpa's* is still there.

Dylan Thomas's ancestors, like my own, have belonged for many generations to this area. A road leads out of X over the back of Lord's Park and in a mile or two comes down, diminished now to a path, at Black Scar, on the remote and desolate flats at the mouth of the river Tâf, opposite the 'heron/Priested shore' and the township of Laugharne. A wild and uninhabited area, the haunt of black-backs, curlews, oyster-catchers, shags and buzzards. Here, in the past, if one wished to cross over the river, which is also wide and tidal, one entered a tiny stone building at the tip of the promontory of Black Scar, and pulled a rope that rang a bell hanging in the roof. One then saw a man leave a cottage on the red cliff-face opposite, get into a boat and punt his way to you across the river. The man was Jack Roberts and his house was the one just below the Boat House where Dylan lived for the last four or five years of his life.

Jack Roberts was an astonishing character, strictly by profession a ferryman and a fisherman. His punt is to be seen in the picture on the back of Dylan's book *A Prospect of the Sea*, with Dylan, Caitlin, and one of the children sitting in it on Laugharne ferry. Sometimes if the tide was low it was necessary in order to get from the bell-house down to Jack's waiting punt, for him to give you a piggyback ride and to plod thus through the sucking mud of the river, sinking almost up to his knees in the revolting squelch at every step. My memories of this mode of transport are bitter and ineradicable because once with me on his back I heard Jack begin to mutter, '*Duw*, *Duw*, I am falling you'. And so it was. Not for the first time in my life, but now literally, I was dropped right in it. I remember Jack also coming around the village of X barefoot and at his customary trot, and crying the fish he carried in his large creel, dabs, flatfish, mostly; but he would never turn back to you if he had passed your door when you wanted to make a purchase. That would have been unlucky, tempting an uncertain fate, and this is something a sea fisherman could not afford to do.

I mentioned earlier the horror which for me existed on the wild seashore beyond Lord's Park. Once when my wife and I were spending a summer holiday in X we saw approaching us one afternoon two dirty, bedraggled, and dishevelled figures, coming wearily up the road towards the house we were staying at. The couple were Dylan and Caitlin, not long married, hungry, thirsty, and exhausted after the exertions of their two-mile scramble; for instead of coming from Laugharne, where they were living, to X by road they had crossed Jack Roberts's ferry and then come along the completely deserted seashore. This way between Black Scar and Wharley Point is an incredibly rough and difficult route. Not even the trace of a pathway exists there between the huge rocks, and the whole bird-whitened, bladderwracked seashore for a mile or two had for me in my romantic adolescence the appearance of a vast deserted playground, where boisterous young Celtic gods had created havoc, playfully hurling at one another the Cyclopean boulders, larger than wardrobes, that are everywhere strewn about the beach or are piled up in massive bastions between the sea and the cliffs from which in the course of the centuries they have fallen.

Only once during my childhood did I venture into this forbidding area. My father, with some of his friends, went there to catch eels, every man armed, ominously and rather thrillingly, with a crowbar. These were both to lever up the rocks under which the eels, left behind by the retreating tide, were said to lurk, and also—every bit as important—to protect oneself against the well-known savagery of these creatures. In the mythology of this myth-ridden area the eels were credited not only with the barks of bloodhounds but also with almost supernatural strength, size, and ferocity. Indeed Willy the Pound once, after an afternoon-long struggle with one of the creatures, staggered into X with the arm-thick monster hanging from his shoulder, impaled through its throat on his crowbar, and its tail dragging in the roadway—and Willy was all of six feet tall!

If someone were to ask me what they could do during a holiday in X I would have to say I haven't the faintest idea. Truthfully, there isn't much one *can* do, except look and listen. Oh, yes, there's bathing (when the tide's in), walking, sea-fishing, horse riding, billiard playing, and cockling, an occupation that is both back-breaking and healthily filthy. But X has no concert hall, no theatre, no cinema, and as far as I know no bingo. The nearest doctor, chemist, dentist, and policeman are probably eight miles away. All this is part of my reluctance to commend X and to state outright its location. To me its charm and beauty are as axiomatic as that the Pope's a Catholic. It is what Dylan Thomas calls 'country heaven' but, to many, its drawbacks and deficiencies might be insufferable. Also a certain tension, an ambivalance, must now exist in one's attitude to any remote and beautiful area to which one has felt long devotion. Love is possessive and on the one hand is the wish to praise, to celebrate, to glorify, and on the other the urge to conserve unaltered, to fight off such awful menaces to peace and sanity as the family car and the transistor radio—even the food-packing indus-try is rapidly approaching this category of horror. Mercifully X is still remote and relatively inaccessible. It has never had a railway line and in my childhood my parents brought me here by boat across the river or by solid-tyred bus from the county town eight miles away. I cannot bring myself to reveal the name of X. The percipient and persistent will no doubt have found many clues to its identity in what I have written. If you, charitable reader as you must necessarily be, follow the clues, please come to X, but come, as I intend always to do myself, in humility and love, so that you might depart in gratitude.

103

Great Britain

JON STALLWORTHY

Out of what depths the dream?
Compounded of what elements? How long
that slow growth, swelling a seam
to ripeness, reconciling
fire and water, earth and air? Under
its own power, now it strikes up, a song
in search of words, a theme for thunder,
overture to a new age, the rising dream of STEAM!

Isambard Kingdom Brunel
heard it above the sounding brass
pounded round a table in Radley's Hotel.
Motions proposed, pass
and fail. Air thickens with the word 'Expand'
scrolled in calculations scrawled by cigars.
'Why should the line end with the land?
Extend it to New York with a steamboat out of Bristol.'

Shipwrights take up the theme,
orchestrating the *Great Western*
till paddle-wheels churn at her beam,
black and white at the stern
shrink to a smudge. Oscillating pistons pound
the sun's track outward, turn and return.
Trumpets sound as a queen is crowned.
Brunel's divining pencil hovers above the dream:

a bridge between old and new,
two piers and a single span
sustaining the traffic of nations. He drew
a line. A second ran
to meet it. Contours of bow, counter and beam
came clear in a flurry of notes. African
oaks crashed to the axe, but the voice of the dream
demanded not timber but iron, not paddles but a screw.

105

With spirit-level and line,
hod and trowel, back and forth,
bricklayers build to Brunel's design
a mammoth womb for a mammoth.
Naysmith works on his steam-hammer, the plate-maker's forge
lights up. Iron seeds jerked from Shropshire earth
enter the crucible, merge, emerge
in a dry dock, marrow cells of a mammoth spine.

Rib after rib now
rises, to be sheathed in an iron skin
by riveters swarming from sternpost to prow,
whose fusillade brings in
the Royal Salute, trumpet and fife and drum.
Ten thousand top hats go off in every direction
at a word from the Prince, who swings a magnum
against the shifting cliff. Lion and Unicorn bow

and lead out, inscrolled
on a trailboard, dove, caduceus, trumpet
and lyre, wheatsheaf and gearwheels of gold.
Roll out the red carpet!
Flags, speak with tongues! Bandmaster, play
Rule Britannia! Fireman, shake sweat
from your eyes and believe them. Say
to your children: 'As God is my witness, the Queen in my
                                        stokehold!'

The heart quickens its beat
and six masts sing as one
as Lion and Unicorn rise to meet
the concerted assault of the ocean;
as the immigrant stands at the stern, tight-lipped;
as the chef in the galley cuts cucumber scales for a salmon;
as the captain writes in a copperplate script
'eleven knots'; and the world turns under their feet.

Great Britain

Eighteen forty-six.
Off-guard, the ship, ripped by the claws
of Dundrum Bay, jarred by its jaws,
    breaks the teeth that transfix
her, throws coal to the sea and scrawls *Help*
on the sky—until dawn calls the tide off. Passengers,
    praising God, flounder through kelp
and bog with their lives in their hands. But the *Great Britain* sticks

    all winter in the Irish gizzard.
Come summer, come levers, come pulleys and weights,
wedges and screw-jacks. A hammer-struck chord
    on ¾ inch plates
leads back the music of the dream. She rises to the tide.
The capstan breaks into song. The cable grates
    as she warps herself off. From Merseyside,
a gun-salute greets the lamed Unicorn's call; and, at Liverpool,
                                                    word

    from Australia: the word was *gold*.
Refitted, rerigged, she takes aboard
the younger son, the crofter, the farmer who sold
    his farm, and plunging southward
holds a long mirror to their dream, that sudden gleam
threading the broken wave. A few of them roared
    with the Forties home, voices of steam
and cigar smoke boasting of bullion in the safe and cotton in the
                                                    hold.

    Iron voices now
break in, trumpet snarling at trumpet,
the battle-cry of the Lion at the bow,
    as jingling files of scarlet
stamp aboard at Liverpool, ashore at Scutari.
Winds threaten. Another course set
    for the Cape and Bombay, she carries a battery
of guns, a squadron of lancers, for Cawnpore and Lucknow.

107

Relics and Locations

The world turns under her keel
  though the screw turns no longer under the wave.
  A windjammer with her holds full of coal,
    she runs for the Horn and the grave
gapes as a hurricane hammers her. Topgallants crack,
  decks leak, and she lists, till her shifting coal
    shovelled uphill, she limps back
To Port Stanley, a listless hulk in her last haven

    but one. *Nineteen-fourteen*.
  Sturdee's ships, loading coal
  from her, stop, as *Scharnhorst* and *Gneisenau* are seen.
    Gruff echoes roll
round the bay, startling the seals, but the Lion never blinks.
  The Unicorn utters no cry, as the scuttling hole
    is struck and the *Great Britain* sinks
in her own reflection. Now circling seabirds keen

    no longer, for she
  has risen, come clear
  of her winding sheet, with all her gear
    shining, as at first he
divined her, Isambard Kingdom Brunel.
  A lesser bard takes up his tune. See here,
    a ship in a bottle, a translucent shell,
that held to the ear inland, remembers the pulse of the sea.

IN THE VILLAGE

They call it regional, this relevance—
the deepest place we have . . .

WILLIAM STAFFORD, *Lake Chelan*

Arrival

R. S. THOMAS

Not conscious
    that you have been seeking
    suddenly
    you come upon it

the village in the Welsh hills
    dust free
    with no road out
but the one you came in by.
    A bird chimes
    from a green tree
the hour that is no hour
    you know. The river dawdles
to hold a mirror for you
where you may see yourself
    as you are, a traveller
    with the moon's halo
    above him, who has arrived
    after long journeying where he
    began, catching this
    one truth by surprise
that there is everything to look forward to.

The Willow-Warblers of the Green

DERWENT MAY

One day last July, I was walking with my eleven-year-old son along the crest of the Malvern Hills. Over to the east lay the great pink and orange plain of England, with only the flat top of Bredon Hill rising above it, a dozen miles away. To the west, Herefordshire and Wales were dark and green and broken. We dipped down now to this side of the crest, now to the other. On the English side it was warm, and the air was still; on the Welsh side the wind blew strong, and our map curved up in our hands as we tried to identify the Welsh peaks. We got cold on that side, so we went back across the path, and sat down in the sunshine on the English slopes.

It was very silent there on the hillside. From far below us, the ringing whine of a circular saw reached us clearly for a while. The dry gorse and bushes, just beneath where we were sitting, seemed empty of life. Then a single bird called softly—'*hooeet*'.

'Willow-warbler,' I said. My son looked up in surprise at something in my tone that he did not recognize.

But no bird's note meant more to me at one time in my life than that half-whispered call. In the summers when I was fifteen and sixteen, all my early mornings and evenings were spent in the company of willow-warblers. My family lived at that time in a Thirties bungalow in a Surrey village called Englefield Green. We inhabited that shapeless boundary where the last suburbs of London mingle with the true countryside. When we moved in, in 1935, the road in front was still not made up; and for all the twenty years we were there, there was a field just behind our neighbours' garden which we called the calf field, since it was used each year as the home of the newly-born calves from the farm a few hundred yards further away. From our garden I could often see a swallow on a telephone wire that ran above the calves' barn.

I started taking an interest in birds when I was about eleven myself, set off in the first place by the desire to win my Naturalist's Badge in the school scout troop. After that, bird-watching quickly became my overwhelming interest in life. And so I got to know the country around Englefield Green with an intimacy that can only come, perhaps, from countless hours of listening to every whistle or twitter in high tree-tops or bramble thickets; from learning to distinguish instantly the flick of a wing from the flutter of a leaf in a windy bush; from creeping along hedges in a posture where the light from the other side will most clearly show up the thickening of the silhouetted foliage which means a nest is hidden there.

A mile away from where I lived there was Windsor Great Park, which, in those wartime days when I best knew it, was a vast, lonely forest. (It has still not changed very much.) Once one was past the lodge at Bishopsgate, where the keeper's garden was adorned with all his old top hats on sticks, one plunged immediately into a deep silent valley of beech trees, oaks, and bracken. A few riders came through, somewhat puzzled by notices saying 'Riders. Please Keep Off These Rides.' Otherwise, winter and summer alike, practically the only sound in this valley, and in the long, forested valleys beyond, was bird sound.

In summer, it might be the sweet, garbled song of redstarts, their tails as red as glowing fire as they swooped across the young ferns. In winter, there were wood-pigeons crashing through twigs in their panic to get into the sky; or the mutter and murmur of little flocks of titmice keeping in contact with each other as they worked through a group of trees; or the sudden explosion of hurried song from a wren, pausing for a moment in a battered tent of dead bracken.

Further into the park, over towards Windsor and Ascot, there were moors, as we called them: broad, tussocky plains, some with heather, where a bird that has since become very rare in England, the woodlark, circled in the sky with a song Shelley should have heard when he lived at Bishopsgate. Then there were the lakes. Virginia Water was drained during the war, for fear that it would be a brilliant landmark for German bombers on moonlit nights. But a friend and I got permits from the Park Ranger's office to visit another stretch of water, Great Meadow Pond, in spite of the fact that Wellington bombers were taking off from one of the 'moors'—Smith's Lawn, now a polo pitch—which was only a few larch-plantations away.

Great Meadow Pond was a haunting place on a winter Sunday morning, which was when we most often went there, since it was a long walk for us and we had no bicycles. It was a big lake, set among woods and cornfields, and edged on three sides by a large area of willow trees and rushes. Through these strange lake borders there ran a system of plank walks, leading out to hides for duck-shooting. There was a breed of water-rabbits that seemed to live in these rushes, and they would go leaping through them, noisily cracking the thin ice, as we tried to go as silently as we could out to the reed-walled shooting-boxes. Sometimes, when we lifted our heads cautiously above the edge of one of the hides, we would surprise gaudy wintering duck—pintails and widgeon—on the water just beneath us; or startle a flock of twenty or thirty teal, that went spinning at incredible speed across the misty surface, then shot up as one into the sky.

Windsor Great Park gave me some of the most memorable experiences I had in those first years of bird-watching. But, in the end, my life centred more on a place nearer home: the Green itself, as it was called, after which Englefield Green was named, and which was only three or four minutes' walk from our house.

Those wartime years were the years when bird-watching became both popular and, to a very considerable degree, scientific. There was a magazine called *British Birds* which I started buying, and in 1943, the year in which I was thirteen, there was published a remarkable book, *The Life of the Robin*, by David Lack. I don't remember how I got hold of this; and of course for me, at that time, its originality wasn't particularly apparent—I took it, like my parents or my school, as something that had more or less always been there. But this little red-bound book became my Bible. It was a detailed account of the author's studies of the annual life-cycle of the robin, which he'd carried out in the local countryside when he was a schoolmaster at Dartington. It was written in a prose that was both scientifically pure, and very graceful and easy. Most important of all for me, it demonstrated how any close study of birds in the wild could contribute quite substantially to our knowledge of them. I looked round for a bird I could watch in the same way, and settled on the willow-warblers of Englefield Green.

The Green—which is, again, still very little changed—began with a broad stretch of grass, with a pub and a pond and a few Georgian houses round the edge of it; then, just beyond, it turned into quite an extensive wood and common. Within its fifteen or so acres, this was a very varied patch of countryside. There were some stretches of open birch wood, mostly young trees, with older ones—their bark both more silvery and more gashed with black—rising here and there above them. There was some thick gorse and bramble common, where the grass was full of lizards and grasshoppers. There were two places with high beech trees, and the usual brown gloom beneath them. I knew virtually every tree and bush, every slight rise and fall of the ground, in this fifteen acres. (One spring, under the beech trees, I noticed a tiny mound among the earth and dead leaves. I bent down and looked at it from ground level, and found the sharp black eyes of a robin on me, staring out of a hole. It was an unusual and risky place for a robin to build its nest, but I remember that the bird hatched successfully, and the brood got away.) I knew how the male linnet swayed, twittering, on a gorse twig, as his mate added a bit of moss to the nest she was building in the depths of the bush; then how she would come shooting out, and the two of them would go looping away together over the gorse tops till they were out of sight. There were chaffinches and white-throats and hedge-sparrows and wrens nesting on the Green. But the most noticeable and beautiful of all the birds on it were the willow-warblers.

They are small olive-green birds, who build a domed nest of grass stalks, usually in a clump of grass at the edge of thin bramble bushes. The males have a very attractive and distinctive song—a run of a dozen or so notes, liquid and silvery, which starts very high and ends almost *sotto voce*. From the first week of April, the birch tops were full of this song. The *'hooeet'* call I spoke of was not heard so much at that time of the year; it was often heard when parents were bringing food to the young, in May and June, or among birds wandering round the countryside after nesting, in July and August—like the one I heard on the Malverns, no doubt.

Armed with David Lack's book as my guide, I started plotting the territories of the willow-warblers on the Green. Male robins hold very clearly defined territories, out of which they drive all other robins, except their mates and their young (and in the autumn they fight with those); willow-warblers, I found, do much the same. I carefully went round the Green hour by hour, in those spring days of 1945 and 1946, marking out the areas occupied by singing males on big maps I made, and slowly coming to feel that I knew the individual birds (I called them A♂, B♂ and so on) and the boundaries they were defending. I found there were about thirty of them, though there were parts of the Green where the situation always remained confused for me—such a flurry of fighting birds, small green wings being flapped in angry display, and gentle song turning into loud and threatening song, that I couldn't distinguish between them with any certainty. In mid-April, the females began to arrive—one morning, I would find a rather subdued but determined new bird in a male's territory, following him around everywhere, being chased off by him from time to time, but slowly being accepted by him under my very eye. Then perhaps the next day they would be feeding together quietly.

This is an essay about a place, rather than about birds, so I will not say much more about willow-warblers. But I must mention their nests, mysterious caves of grass, their entrance no larger than a half-crown, their interiors lined with white feathers—wood-pigeon down, very often. Sometimes I would gently ease an egg to the front of the nest with my little finger, and roll it into the palm of my other hand—a tiny white egg, ringed with dull red spots or blurs. 'Puggers'—boys who took eggs, or smashed nests—were my enemies as a bird-watcher in the village, but they mainly scoured the hedgerows, and hardly ever thought of looking on the ground for willow-warblers' nests. So most of the eggs hatched, and in a fortnight there were four or five plump green birds waiting to fly. I did once move a pair of lovers who were lying so close to a nest I thought they might roll on to it, while the parents were *hooeet*ing anxiously in the branches nearby. I took a chance and showed the couple the nest, to explain my intervention, and luckily they expressed great interest, then found another place. To conclude the story—I eventually wrote an article for *British Birds* on the willow-warblers of Englefield Green, then a longer one for another ornithological journal called *Ibis*. And I met David Lack in due course, working for him for a few months, before I went into the Army, at the Edward Grey Institute of Field Ornithology in Oxford. That gave me the desire to go up to Oxford as an undergraduate, and so set my life off on a new course. But I was already changing. I remember, about that time, saying to a friend, 'You know, that descending cadence of the willow-warbler's song is like a silk garment slipping off a shoulder.' 'I see you've got new interests,' he said.

But the Park and the Green have always remained with me, and the knowledge I acquired at the time has never quite gone. When I came back to England after three years in Indonesia, I went soon afterwards on a train to Oxford. While the train was standing in a country station, I noticed a faint movement at the top of a tree. I couldn't say it was a movement *of* anything: it was quite abstract. But I said to myself, 'That's the movement of a magpie flirting his tail.' And as the train pulled out of the station, and the sunlit side of the tree came into view, there was a black and white magpie sitting upright and shining on a high bough.

What is more, the Green and the Park form a kind of axis from which all my feelings about the countryside still take their measure. The birds—and the trees and flowers—that were common there when I was a boy are still those that I greet as natural friends; whereas those that were uncommon or rare still surprise me when I see them. In London, nowadays, there are far more greenfinches than chaffinches. But greenfinches were rare in Englefield Green, and when I see them flying sturdily over Camden Town, I still look up at them with astonishment, and a sense of new pleasure. Meanwhile, London ornithologists go round making careful records of every singing chaffinch, while I pass them by as a commonplace background.

So it was on that Malvern hillside. We got up and went on our way along the unfamiliar track towards Worcestershire Beacon. For me, as for my son, there were fine, fresh sensations at every dip and rise of that strange outcrop of hills. But the willow-warbler's voice had added something else. This, too, was England; this, too, was home.

A Year in West Oxfordshire

Barbara Pym

About twelve miles west of Oxford, in the Wychwood Forest area on the edge of the Cotswolds, is a cluster of remote villages off the main tourist track. Few of these villages would win a prize for tidiness and elegance, and some of them even now have an air of romantic decay, dating from the depressed Thirties (when my own village, Finstock, was described by one visitor as 'a tattered hamlet', and by another as being imbued with an evil emanation from the forest). Today there is an interesting mixture of carefully restored cottages and bright new bungalows with broken dry-stone walls, corrugated iron, and nettles, and even the occasional deserted or ruined homestead.

Every writer probably keeps some kind of diary or notebook, and

119

my own (mercifully less personal and introspective as the years go on) has provided these few observations on the weather and natural surroundings, history and literary associations of the area.

January. Cold, snow, and blizzard and from my window I can watch cars failing to get up the hill to Wilcote. Later in the month a visit to Swinbrook, a pretty, well-kept village. In the church the Fettiplaces lie on their stone shelves—the mansion where they lived was demolished early in the last century and the family has now died out. But Swinbrook still has its Mitford associations—a tablet to Tom Mitford in the church, and the graves of Nancy and Unity in the churchyard. Go to Asthall nearby and stand in the churchyard to look at the manor where the Mitfords lived as children.

February. Sometimes a mild, false spring. The month for gathering firewood in the forest (and once finding half of a deer's antler).

March. (Roses should be pruned by the end of this month.) On the 21st the first day of official 'summer' with its bleak, cold-light evening. A good walk from Finstock, up the hill to Wilcote (with grey-stone Wilcote House, not all quite as old as it looks, and the apricot-washed manor), past the little romantic-looking church, then down to Ramsden, a more beautiful village than Finstock. Meanly trying to find examples of 'direness' (ugly bungalows, corrugated iron, nettles and general squalor), but it is less in evidence here than in other villages in these parts. The main street is pretty and orderly, but you seldom see people walking about.

April. Four kittens born in time for a fine warm Easter. On Low Sunday 'reviving' the Easter decorations in the church. Some of the daffodils have survived in the chilly atmosphere (no central heating). Finstock Church is neither ancient nor particularly beautiful, but it has the distinction of being the place where T. S. Eliot was received into the Church of England on 29 June 1927. A bronze plaque to commemorate this has been put up in the church and was dedicated by the Bishop of Oxford on 23 June 1974. There is an account of Eliot's baptism in *T. S. Eliot: A Memoir*:*

William (Force Stead) was living some fifteen miles distant from Oxford in a fine, seventeenth-century gabled house at Finstock on the borders of

* By Robert Sencourt, ed. Donald Adamson. Garnstone Press (1971) p. 109.

Essex Granary by Charles Hall

Wychwood Forest. He arranged that Tom should come and stay with him there and meet two friends who were to be his godfathers (B. H. Streeter and Vere Somerset). On the afternoon of 29th June 1927, St. Peter's Day, William met with his three guests and locked the doors of the little church at Finstock before pouring the water of regeneration over the head of one who in future years was to be as much the leading layman in the Church of England as Lord Halifax was at that time.

William Force Stead, I believe, was a chaplain at one of the Oxford colleges. There are some lines in *Little Gidding* which are said to refer to this event. Only which ones, I wonder? Perhaps these:

> Thus, love of a country
> Begins as attachment to our own field of action
> And comes to find that action of little importance
> Though never indifferent. History may be servitude,
> History may be freedom. See, now they vanish,
> The faces and places, with the self which, as it could,
> loved them,
> To become renewed, transfigured, in another pattern.

May. In a good year this is the best month in this part of the country. Buttercups, cow parsley, and sun. And, of course, the cuckoo (A. E. Housman's poem, 'The cuckoo shouts all day at nothing/In leafy dells alone . . .'). And, if it isn't too hot, a walk up to Wilcote and a beautiful 'sepia' portrait of sheep grazing in the churchyard round the tombstones. Another walk in Patch Riding, on the edge of the forest going into Cornbury Park (though you can't go into the Park). The bluebells will be out and towards the end of the month you can sometimes see bluebells and wild garlic out together.

June. The most variable month of the year—hottest, coldest, wettest. The eleventh is St. Barnabas's (Hymn 222 in the English Hymnal, by Mrs Maude Coote—'The Son of Consolation!/Of Levi's priestly line . . .'. A walk up to the church for evensong (poorly attended these days). The Collect for St. Barnabas, who came from Cyprus and who introduced St. Paul to the new church at Jerusalem, says that he was endued with 'singular gifts' and asks God not to leave us 'destitute of thy manifold gifts'. Barnabas was with the disciples at Antioch, the place where the word 'Christians' was first used.

A Year in West Oxfordshire

July. This year (1979) summer at last! Garden full of honey-suckle, syringa, roses (June is hardly ever the month of roses in this garden). Later in this month the almost overwhelming scent of elder-flowers. Sitting in front of the cottage in the early evening, looking at the light on a creamy-grey stone barn opposite, seeing down the hill from Wilcote a hay cart (motorized now, of course!) approaching—huge rolls of hay are the fashion now—said to be easier, more convenient, for the cows to eat. As the hot weather goes on, especially with this year's wet spring and early summer, the countryside becomes 'luxuriant'—luscious grass and uncut hedgerows with the scabious coming out, and many weeds in the garden, almost a plague of self-seeded violets. Excursion to Rousham, a Jacobean house, redecorated mid-eighteenth century by William Kent who also designed the landscape and the gar-dens—temples, follies, terraces, grottoes, and sculptures, and a view down the river. On a summer Saturday you might be the only people there, with the pigeons (Norwich Croppers) in the seventeenth-century dovecote, and bantams with feathered legs.

August. This month Ditchley Park is open to the public. The poet John Wilmot, Earl of Rochester, was born here in 1647. His poems are hymns—to girls.

> My light thou art—without thy glorious sight
> My eyes are darken'd with eternal night.
> My Love, thou art my way, my life, my light.
>
> Thou art my way; I wander if thou fly.
> Thou art my light; if hid, how blind am I!
> Thou art my life; if thou withdraw'st, I die.

According to John Evelyn, it was in Rochester's day 'a low timber house with a pretty bowling green', but now it is larger and more imposing, turned into a conference centre. Churchill used to stay here during the war when it was owned by the late Ronald Tree. He was an American who bought the house from Lord Dillon in 1933. Tree described his first view of it in his book *When the Moon was High*:*

I remember the hedges on either side of the road being full of wild roses and honeysuckle, and the smell of the new-mown hay. A few minutes later we

---

* p. 37. Macmillan (1975).

came out of the lane and before us was the great double avenue of beech trees leading up the lodge gate. I remember that first sight of it: we marvelled at it. Once through the gates we found ourselves in a heavily wooded park where the deer, many of them white, were grazing or lying in the bracken, their little heads turning enquiringly towards the car as we passed. Ahead, another avenue of elm trees, and then the house itself appeared, stark grey against the blue sky, its two lead statues of Loyalty and Fame looking far out over the trees towards the Churchill Palace at Blenheim, its neighbour to the east.

The poet Rochester and his family are buried in the vaults of Spelsbury church, but there is no tablet to record his memory. The beautiful monument you will see in this church is to the third Earl of Lichfield (1776) who also lived at Ditchley. In the churchyard outside is the large square-oblong tomb where the Cary family are said to be buried, but the top is broken and there is a scattering of bones (can they be human bones?), dry and grey-white. The grass in the churchyard bleached creamy-white and a distant view of what look like downs (though they can't be).

September. This is the month of plums and jam-making, beans and the last courgettes and tomatoes ripening in the garden. (A London friend doesn't appreciate the courgettes, so carefully nurtured and proudly tended, thinks them 'tasteless'—and may well criticize the tomatoes of which one is equally proud.) And of course September is the great blackberry month and the lanes round here are full of them.

October. This is still a good blackberry month and they are often at their best, but after a certain date (I can't remember exactly which) they are said to belong to the Devil, or even (in some parts) the Devil is thought to be in them! This is usually the month for Harvest Festival, though the harvest is gathered in earlier—much fruit and flowers in the church, of course, but one year it was noted that vegetables were 'not given sufficient prominence in the decorations'. (What is Harvest Festival without at least one enormous marrow?) For a change you could go to South Leigh church (St. James's) where a nineteenth-century vicar (Gerard Moultrie) made the translation from the Greek of the magnificent Communion hymn which is No. 318 in the English Hymnal. It is called the Liturgy of St. James.

Let all mortal flesh keep silence
And with fear and trembling stand;
Ponder nothing earthly-minded,
For with blessing in his hand
Christ our God to earth descendeth,
Our full homage to demand.

A nostalgic visit to the Trout Inn at Wolvercote for a memory of Oxford days in the Thirties. Guinness and sandwiches outside—eight peacocks but no trace of the wisteria of forty years ago. Now red creeper and what looks like a vine. A man and a girl embracing by the river, so nothing changes all that much. Huge car park.

November. Still a few roses in the garden and even on the altar in church. The first iris stylosa may begin to come out so that you have the remains of summer and (perhaps) spring, though there's probably a lot of winter to be got through before then.

December. Hyacinths coming out in the house. Gathering and sawing wood for the fire is good exercise. A grey-white sky and a bleak landscape—plenty of bare trees but the death of the elms has left many gaps. Christmas seems suddenly mild and green, and as the days gradually lighten you begin to look forward to starting the year in West Oxfordshire all over again.

Wickhamford Church, Vale of Evesham, Worcestershire, 1925

JAMES LEES-MILNE

By the evening it has stopped raining and is fine again. The sun is almost on the horizon. It is sweeping down the lane between the poor hedgerows of alder and blackthorn, broken hedgerows repaired at intervals with stakes and withies cut from the bank of the brook by the old bridge, where the lane makes a kink in its passage and in winter clogs the wheels of the horse drays; is sweeping through the lank hemlock along the verges, the hemlock which in summer bows and sways in the wake of the rattling horse drays; overflowing into the market gardens on either side and inundating the serried furrows of cabbage and asparagus fern; percolating through the orchard of Worcester apples where the grass is long now but where in springtime the daffodils attract the charabanc trippers from Birmingham; gliding through the patulous leaves of the sycamore on the green, and through the drive gates of my old home; spluttering through the acacia tree by the kitchen window; splashing a way through the branches of the chestnut trees opposite; churning a way through the gravel of the drive and settling with a bang on Tyko, the bull-terrier rolled up like a whiting and yawning on the rubber mat with MAT perforated across it, before the front door of the manor house at Wickhamford.

The sun is almost on the horizon. The evening air is so still and strange that each sound falls clear like the last raindrops after a storm, whether the starlings' raucous shrieks, the beating of egg yolk with a wire whisk behind the kitchen window, the roar of the Paddington express down the straight bit of track from Honeybourne to Badsey three miles away, or the hum of life from the market town, rolling round the hollow at the end of the lane and carried along the flat sunbeams.

I have been reading indoors. Closing my book I saunter through the hall and, stepping over Tyko's white body, stroll down the drive. The gravel crunches under my feet with a noise of exploding rockets. I shield the sun from my eyes with my book. I shut the wooden gates, pass through the orchard and turn into the churchyard.

I amble slowly up the church pathway with the sunset behind me. The air is opalescent and the sky ahead where it drops to touch the wall bounding the churchyard and the manor garden is a violet curtain of unwrinkled velvet, so close that I am tempted to put out a hand to stroke it. The stalks of the mauve valerian sprouting from the jagged wall-coping are a stitched embroidery hem responsive to the pads of my fingers running over them.

'Sacred to the Memory', I read, 'of John Taylor', 'Amelia Pethard', 'Hannah Bean', and 'Annie Hacklett'. Sacred to the memory of eternal generations of men, women, and children, born, bred, propagating and dead, at Wickhamford since Time began. All dead to themselves while living, dead to the world today, and only alive to me. All alive to me, I ruminate, halting and peering at a tomb-

Headley, Surrey by Kenneth Scowa

stone sunk in the soft earth and settled upon the grave, six foot down, of an elm-wood coffin once hacked from Wickhamford trees and now fossilized by stiff clay; perished but firm like the ribs and struts of Caligula's warship, only kept in place by the weight and survival of the lead lining, cast into endurance by the molten hammer blows of Worcestershire farriers, preserving until Judgement Day the undisturbed shreds of bone, flesh, and cerecloth stuck to the lead bottom and recognizable to God as the contours and figments of a human carcass.

'Sacred to the Memory' I read again while making for the porch and catching the sweet scent of hay yielded by the dead and the tinkle of the fountain the far side of the velvet curtain, coming from my father's sunken garden.

I halt under the porch where layers of tattered notices, absurdly headed 'Income Tax' in bold, black type, are curling at the four corners, and only kept in place on the baize notice-board by a rusty drawing pin which bruises the vicar's fingernails after matins on the third Sunday of each month. Next to them and impinged upon a bent hook flutter list upon list of the amounts, including a detailed record of half-crown, florin, shilling, sixpenny, threepenny, penny, halfpenny, and even farthing pieces, contributed to the weekly collection bag. These lists which, save on Festival Sundays and especially on Easter Day, cunningly reveal to the curious through their exiguous totals that the manor pew is too frequently empty, are faithfully compiled under their several headings by old Mrs Hartwell, verger and sexton in one.

The handle of the church door presents difficulties to the uninitiated. With the precision born of familiarity I grasp the fat iron ring, kidney-shaped, in both hands, push inward the bolt to which it is attached and turn it towards the direction of the lock. The door, made of thick oak boards medievally clamped together with nails and studs of the rudest workmanship swings open heavily, shouting a discord of resentment and discontent.

I descend two steps into the nave, closing the door behind me, fearful of its weight upon the flimsy staples in the masonry that hinges it. I am alone, inhaling the beetle dust from the dry oak rafters, the must from the vellum pages of Prayer Books with nap calf bindings, the starch from the vicar's surplice in the vestry, and the oil from the brass lamps suspended from tie-beams and defining scrolls and twirls of art nouveau metalwork against the white plaster walls.

My eyes soon accustom themselves to the religious light now struggling through the greeny-white panes of the west window from the sun, dead on the horizon and hampered by the trees of Worcester apples in the orchard, the sun just trickling on to the unornamented font with a common cork in the plug hole.

I am alone, I assure myself, clutching my book, accustoming my eyes to the dimness, my limbs to the charnel cool of the interior which I love. Here I am one with the history of Wickhamford, where time stands still and the pageantry of the past is petrified in the present. Here the history of the manor is unfurled about me. I can reach out and grasp the lineage of the old squires like a long mantle sewn with the lozenges of heraldic heiresses without number, stitched in battle silk thread of Plantagenet tinctures, upon fields of York white and Lancaster red.

I pass the high box-pews and double-decker pulpit, in the little oak niches of which stand stiff ranks of saints, their heads chopped off by Cromwell's soldiers. Here is the plush drapery of the reading desk upon which the vicar spills candle grease while lighting the charred wicks, peering over his spectacles and galloping through the absolution, all at the same moment. And there is the manor pew, with a crest on the door panel, and long velvet squabs, with moth holes in them, upon the upright benches.

The nave has by now become dank and chilly. Grey tails of dusk are frisking about it. I leave the nave and pass under the rood arch, upon which are faintly traceable the painted arms and supporters of Restoration England and the date 1661 that has subsequently been touched up. I pass through the oak gates, beeswax grey, into the chancel.

I enter the Holy of Holies, where there is more colour, where the leaves of the chestnut trees flit like bats' wings behind the glowing lancet windows. I am at the steps of the altar and these are the rails beyond which I should not go. Here are the Caroline monuments to the squires of Wickhamford, husbands with wives, sons with daughters-in-law.

On the north side of the chancel is a fair double monument of alabaster, supported by five pillars of touchstone and ornamented above with the

statues of Faith, Hope, Charity and Time. Whereon lieth Sir Samuel
Sandys armed, and praying, his head and hands bare, at his feet a cocka-
trice; by him his lady, her hands joined as in prayer; at her feet on a wreath
argent and azure an arpine's head argent, with his horns, mane and beard,
or. Over them their arms. The first escutcheon, gules a bend dancetté,
between as many cross crosslets fitchée or, for Sandys. The second
escutcheon all Culpeper's coat gules in a lozenge.

This is how the county historian describes them in his Georgian
heraldic prose.

Silent and solemn, fathers and sons, mailed in archaic armour,
the veins of their slender hands and the tips of their conjoined
fingers, the lineaments of their oval faces, the trimming of their
pointed beards, the curls of their cavalier locks, the lids of their
closed eyes and the impress of their heads on creased cushions with
tassels of gold, are carved in alabaster—living ghosts of the ancient
families of Sandys and Culpeper, Bulkeley and Pakington, Kidwally
and Carthorpe, Throckmorton and Patshull.

Blockley, Gloucestershire

WILLIAM TREVOR

When I think of landscape which is special I find myself back in the
County Cork of my childhood. But the Brits haven't ruled there for
generations now, so I must start again. As a child in Youghal and
Skibbereen—poor little towns in those days—I wondered about
England: there was a Royal Family, Henry Hall on the wireless,
important weddings in the *Daily Sketch*. England spelt elegance,
and style and graciousness. It had a capital city so huge that I was
assured it would stretch all the way from Skibbereen to Cork City.
Occasionally a G.B. car went by, always gleaming, grey or black. If
it stopped by the roadside a picnic would take place, a special little
kettle placed on a primus stove, sponge cake brought in a tin box
from Surrey. Accents were polished, ladies kindly smiled. One of
them gave me a fig-roll once.

Elms by John Trelawny-Ross

There was a board-game we played, long before Monopoly. It had to do with train journeys up and down England, all of them beginning at railway stations that had a magic ring: Paddington, Victoria, Waterloo, King's Cross. 'Gloucestershire?' my father said. 'It's a county. Like County Cork or County Wexford.' If you were lucky with your dice you might hurry away by G.W.R. to Gloucestershire, while others were stuck *en route* to Huddersfield or Belper. I imagined a leafy place, nice for picnics, threads of gold among the green. It spread itself out like a tapestry in my mind: nothing was ruined there, no burnt-out houses or smashed castles, no brambles growing through rusty baronial gates as we had in County Cork. The Duke of Gloucester would never have permitted that.

Many years later, when I was in my early twenties but still had not once left Ireland, I came a little closer to Gloucestershire, told about it by the girl I was to marry: about the Slaughters and the Swells, and Adlestrop and Evenlode, in particular about the village of Blockley. That Cotswold world began in marvellous, onion-domed Sezincote, one of Gloucestershire's stately homes which in 1939 briefly became a haven from German bombs. Afterwards there was a cottage in Blockley itself: Little Manor, a bit overgrown these days, opposite the smart new restaurant which has put the village on the gastronomic map.

For being told about this part of England made me want to visit it and returning now, I find my childhood vision of an orderly dukedom shattered yet again: it's the hard years of war that come rushing back on a warm July afternoon. Cycling to the grammar school in Chipping Campden, taking the wet batteries to be charged, that's where Miss Tavender lived, that's cruel Fish Hill where you pushed your bike for a mile. The three great houses—Northwick Park and Batsford as well as Sezincote—cannot be as once they were, nor is Sleepy Hollow or Donkey Lane. And Rock Cottage, where that doubtful prophetess Joanna Southcott spent the last ten years of her life, has been burnt down. But leeks still thrive in the garden that was Sergeant Wall's, and Rose of Sharon in old Mrs Whale's. A pear-tree still decorates a façade in St. George's Terrace, the house called Rodneys is still the smartest. Irises and lacy delphiniums prosper, valerian sprouts from the cracks in soft brown walls. Old-fashioned roses are everywhere.

In wartime Blockley there were Italian prisoners of war, laughing while they mended the roads. American soldiers eyed the solitary wives and gave a party for their children, real paste in the sandwiches. 'Aluminium for the war effort!' these same children cried from door to door, taking it in turn to push the pram. They came away with broken saucepans, and between his dozes on a sunny step the village fat boy watched and was amused. He watched as drowsily when the bull ran madly down the long main street, and again when Mrs Jones was dragged the length of it by her husband, unexpectedly home on leave. He watched while villagers brought Mr French a single egg so that he could bake them a cake in Half Crown Cottage. He listened without pleasure while Mr Lunn consoled himself with Bach, or roused himself to warn against the churchyard in the black-out, his thin voice telling of its restless dead.

Blockley nestles, as Broad Campden does, and Shipston on Stour. The wolds encase them: lazy undulations, fields guarded by trim stone walls. Patches of sheep whiten the hilly sward, poppies blaze through a field of rye. In the July sunshine the roadside verges are a yard high, yellowing cow-parsley sprinkled with crane's-bill and campion. Elder fills the hedgerows.

In Stow on the Wold you pass down an ancient passage to the Gents, and the hard black oak of door-frames seems tougher than the ubiquitous stone. Above hotels and pubs the wrought-iron signs are motionless on a tranquil afternoon. 'The real McCoy!' an American cyclist proclaims, pausing in one town or another, it doesn't matter which. Tea-rooms are full of shortbread and Bendicks' chocolate mint crisps, part of the scenery.

Domestic pastoral: the Cotswold scene is that, the stone of houses is the stone of the wolds, and Cotswold faces are part of nature too. At dusk, old women in summer dresses make the journey through their village to look at someone else's flowers. At dawn, unshaven itinerants move dourly through the fields from one farm to the next. With passing years, these small conventions remain, even if Northwick Park has become a business school and Blockley's silk mills are bijou residences now. The Gloucestershire voice hasn't altered much, either: on market day in Moreton in Marsh it's matter-of-fact and firm, without the lilt that sweetens it further west. Like the countryside it speaks for, its tones are undramatic, as if constantly aware that life owes much to sheep, that least theatrical of animals. While landscape and buildings merge, nobody who lives here is likely to forget that the riches and good sense of wool merchants created the Cotswolds.

When I walk in England I walk in Dartmoor or Derbyshire, and I have chosen Devon to live in. I like the English seaside out of season, Budleigh Salterton and Bexhill; it is Somerset I watch playing cricket. But best of all in England there's Gloucestershire to visit and to stroll through, while pheasants rise elegantly from its parklands and rivers modestly make their way. No matter how remote or silent a wood may be there's always a road or a person within reach: I think of Tennyson when I walk in Gloucestershire, the way that runs through the field, two lovers lately wed, an abbot on an ambling pad. I think as well of old Mrs Whale in her lifetime and Sergeant Wall in his, of Albert the footman at Sezincote, Miss Tavender a schoolmistress, and Joanna Southcott. Blockley Brass Band still performs, weather permitting; there are outings to distant Ramsgate. 'Dubious Dog Contest' the sign outside the British Legion hall announces, and I imagine the pink tongues panting on a Saturday afternoon, setters and spaniels that aren't quite the thing, terriers that should have been Dalmatians. The children of the children who ate the American soldiers' paste sandwiches self-consciously tug the leashes. The sun has brought the hollyhocks out.

The countryside is the setting, but people come first: in spite of disturbance and change it is that that continues, and returning now I feel my childhood instinct was not far wrong. In this warm July, or in their wartime years, in snow or sun, the wolds are unique; and their towns and villages perfectly complement them. Crowded with hastening tourists, all three retain their essence: England is unstifled here.

BOROUGH
BOUNDARIES

Look at the stars! look, look up at the skies!
O look at all the fire-folk sitting in the air!
The bright boroughs, the circle-citadels there!

GERARD MANLEY HOPKINS, *The Starlight Night*

Connemara, Galway by John Piper

Here

Philip Larkin

Swerving east, from rich industrial shadows
And traffic all night north; swerving through fields
Too thin and thistled to be called meadows,
And now and then a harsh-named halt, that shields
Workmen at dawn; swerving to solitude
Of skies and scarecrows, haystacks, hares and pheasants,
And the widening river's slow presence,
The piled gold clouds, the shining gull-marked mud,

Gathers to the surprise of a large town:
Here domes and statues, spires and cranes cluster
Beside grain-scattered streets, barge-crowded water,
And residents from raw estates, brought down
The dead straight miles by stealing flat-faced trolleys,
Push through plate-glass swing doors to their desires—
Cheap suits, red kitchen-ware, sharp shoes, iced lollies,
Electric mixers, toasters, washers, driers—

A cut-price crowd, urban yet simple, dwelling
Where only salesmen and relations come
Within a terminate and fishy-smelling
Pastoral of ships up streets, the slave museum,
Tattoo-shops, consulates, grim head-scarfed wives;
And out beyond its mortgaged half-built edges
Fast-shadowed wheat-fields, running high as hedges,
Isolate villages, where removed lives

Loneliness clarifies. Here silence stands
Like heat. Here leaves unnoticed thicken,
Hidden weeds flower, neglected waters quicken,
Luminously-peopled air ascends;
And past the poppies bluish neutral distance
Ends the land suddenly beyond a beach
Of shapes and shingle. Here is unfenced existence:
Facing the sun, untalkative, out of reach.

Bulwell

STANLEY MIDDLETON

Bulwell where I was born has been a suburb of Nottingham for more than a hundred years now, but the people affect not to notice it. It took its name from a spring where a careless Saxon bull stabbed the rock with its horn (as illustrated in a carving above the door of the church school on Main Street), and any mention of the name in the Christmas pantomime at the Theatre Royal four miles away would raise an instant laugh. There lived the barbarians who mangled the language as they had done since Domesday; there lived the blackened miners (we called them 'colliers') and the bleachers who fought in the pubs or sang in the chapels, and both with a desperate disrespect for moderation.

The town lies in a valley, and through it flows the Leen which would run mad from time to time to excite us and flood the Main Street. The river's course is short from Newstead Abbey to a dull end under cover in the Trent. The hills round about are low, but obvious, and seemed peculiarly suitable to the Nonconformity under which I was brought up. 'The hills that gird our dwellings round,' we sang, 'As Thou dost gird Thine own with love' exactly described us, so that we spoke correctly of going 'up park' when we went to the cricket field, and arrogantly of travelling 'down Notts' when we went to the city, though the tramcars began the journey with a grind up Church Hill. Nottingham with its castle seemed a long way off like our other pleasure-spots such as the Trent or Skegness, and we'd demotically express surprise by 'I'll goo t'Trent Bridge' as well, paradoxically, as 'I'll go t'our 'ouse'.

There the town crouched, then, in its hollow. When I became a reader and discovered D. H. Lawrence, born not five miles away as the crow flies, the effect was startling. And much as I resented his 'miserable Bulwell' in *Strike Pay* he more than made up for it with a sentence in *Sons and Lovers*, a sentence I greatly admired and often copied: '. . . there was a patch of lights at Bulwell like myriad petals shaken to the ground from the shed stars; and beyond was the red glare of the furnaces, playing like hot breath on the clouds'. Not that we were a literary community; that Lord Byron was buried in

the parish church of the next township, Hucknall Torkard, mattered to us not at all until they dug him up and found the body undecayed. That was more interesting than his poetry.

The cottages along the Quarry Road were built of a golden stone, hewn locally, and even some of the main shops (once one lifted one's eyes from the disfiguring fronts) were similar. So were the chapels, though these had darkened, and the Victorian, square-towered church on its hillock. The rector there once electrified me by claiming (we'd been taken in a crocodile from school up to St. Mary's on Ascension Day) that he'd actually seen an angel flit across the west end. His hand traced the flight. He made the claim without stress, in his Anglican voice. In our Wesleyan Chapel there were plenty who knew the way of the Lord, and were not averse to making it plain to you, but they never saw an angel. They would have said so, for sure. I appeared at the age of nine with the same rector on the boards of the Olympia, our theatre, in a pageant of scenes from old Bulwell, and represented, I hope uncharacteristically, a prize pupil of the grammar school, with a recitation to him of:

> Her eyes were as bright as the pips of a pear;
> No rose in the garden with her lips could compare;
> Her hair hung in ring-a-lets, all beautiful and long;
> I thought that she loved me, but I found I was wrong.

The old school building still exists, a beautiful, small house in rustic brick surrounded by low walls, with a treed garden and its date, 1667, over the door with the Strelley arms, in the criss-cross of streets of early twentieth-century terraces.

We were never short of eccentrics, odd men who lived their own way. On the cricket field a fanfare on the concertina greeted a boundary from the home side, while a straight six on to the cowshed roof of the farm nearby guaranteed an outburst of Mahlerian length and strength. There was Jack Arlott (if he spelt himself with an 'h' it was never pronounced) who, in gnarled middle-age, terrified and delighted the girls at night with his question-and-answer: 'A' you 'eard? Ah'm gerrin' married.' My brother and his friends regularly scattered screaming lasses with their imitation in the lamp-lit streets. We were cruel, I suspect, to abnormality, and scared. I remember as a small boy standing for some minutes in the open market-place, naphtha flares dowsed, booths folded, in the dark of the evening, watching a man who leaned on a deserted stall, his nose dripping blood into a puddle on the ground. No one was with him; he made no attempt to staunch the flow; if he saw me, he gave no sign. He bled in silence.

When I think back to childhood I suffer as English townspeople have for the past hundred and fifty years, I suspect, from the fear that we are madly building over all our fields. The top of the street where I lived, terraced houses on a fine, left-curving, cobbled road, was blocked by a high stone wall. True, some vandal or benefactor had knocked a hole in it, but beyond it were allotments and dirt-lanes, and what my father called 'gillivers' grew in the niches of the wall. Perhaps the land belonged to the squire, I cannot say, and he wanted to keep the plebs out. One could only reach nearby Hazel Street, where the frame-knitters had once lived and starved, through a narrow 'jitty', and Merchant Street not at all. The City Corporation had now bought the park, but the eighteenth-century hall stood, as sanatorium or approved school, until after the Second World War. Old people remembered the squire's lady pushing her way with not so much as a by-your-leave into your pantry in times of scarcity. If shelves were bare, relief was despatched immediately, but there was no mercy for those with a rabbit knocked-off for the pot. I could never tell whether these women, with old-fashioned names like Emma and Sarah Jane, admired such behaviour or disapproved. We Bulwellians were independent, we said, but when Jeremiah Brandreth, the Captain from Nottingham, fled here after the Pentrich Rising of 1817, his friend, one Sansom, found the reward too tempting and handed him over to armed gamekeepers for trial, hanging, and beheading. It was in the hall park, with its woods and grassy mounds, that people courted and died. We heard of suicides in the ponds, and searched for evidence of the lightning which killed a girl under a tree in the hawthorn hedge lining the road.

But it is the common land, the 'Forest', I remember best; it seemed a 'high place' with its bright sandstone, and gorse, and harebells and silver birches, and though it was, then as now, a golf-course, few people played during the daytime. Its small hollows had their own names; we sledged, for instance, down Nick Dale. Here on a Sunday afternoon, no golfers about, the world promenaded in its best, staring out towards Annesley Church, exchanging greetings or insults. Only cross the road, push under the bridge by the wagon-works, and one was on the Duke of St. Albans' estate, rising farmland, a different country. But the common was at its best at night, in winter, when the wind shredded clouds across the moon, and smoke blew and shifted from every chimney down in the valley, over the viaduct, the factories, the black humps of the chapels, slate roofs wet and shining. Here was a fit place to walk, scarfed, and look out over the railway line to London, and nurse ambition.

The New Cemetery

NORMAN NICHOLSON

Now that the town's dead
Amount to more than its calculable future,
They are opening a new graveyard

In the three-hedged field where once
Horses of the L.M.S. delivery wagons
Were put to grass. Beside the fence

Of the cricket-ground we'd watch
On Saturday afternoon, soon after the umpires
Laid the bails to the stumps and the match

Had begun. They'd lead them
Then between railway and St. George's precinct—huge
Beasts powerful as the steam

Engines they were auxiliary to:
Hanked muscles oscillating slow and placid as pistons,
Eyes blinkered from all view

Of the half-acre triangle of green,
Inherited for Sunday. But once they'd slipped the harness,
And the pinched field was seen

The New Cemetery

With its blue lift of freedom,
Those haunches heaved like a sub-continental earthquake
Speeded up in film.

Half a ton of horse-flesh
Rose like a balloon, gambolled like a week-old lamb;
Hind legs lashed

Out at inoffensive air,
Capsized a lorryful of weekdays, stampeded down
Fifty yards of prairie.

We heard the thump
Of hoof on sun-fired clay in the hush between
The bowler's run-up

And the click of the late
Cut. And when, one end-of-season day, they lead me
Up through the churchyard gate

To that same
Now consecrated green—unblinkered and at last delivered
Of a lifetime's

Load of parcels—let me fling
My hooves at the boundary wall and bang them down again,
Making the thumped mud ring.

Barchester Lives On

Jan Morris

Searching on a wistful whim for Barchester, I came to Wells in Somerset. I craved the Trollopian scene not for itself exactly, but for its myth of a Golden Age. Of course I wanted the incidentals too, the bells across the close, the fine old ladies taking tea beneath college rowing groups featuring, at stroke, their uncle the late Precentor. I wanted the mingled smell of dry rot and market cabbage. I hoped to catch a glimpse of the Organist and Choirmaster, pulling his gown over his shoulders as he hurried across to evensong. But like many other romantics, all over the western world, I hungered really for the hierarchical certainty of the old England, that amalgam of faith, diligence, loyalty, independence and authority which Trollope mischievously enshrined in the legends of his little city.

At least Wells looks impeccably the part. As one descends from the spooky heights of Mendip, haunted by speleologists and Roman snails, it lies there in the lee of the hills infinitely snug and wholesome. No motorway thunders anywhere near. It is fourteen miles to the nearest railway station. Though Wells has been a city since the tenth century, it is still hardly more than an ample village, dutifully assembled around the towers of the cathedral: and though beyond it one may see the arcane bumps and declivities of the Glastonbury plain, there is nothing very mystical to one's first impression of the place. Its accent is homely Somerset, and its aspect rubicund.

In no time at all I had found myself a room, low-beamed and flower-patterned, in the Crown Hotel overlooking the Market Square, where a rivulet swims limpidly down the gutter past the old town conduit: and hardly less promptly, as it happened, I found myself fined £2 for parking too long outside Penniless Porch, through whose squinted archway the green of the precinct had too soon enticed me, and above whose tower and great grey mass of the cathedral itself looked benignly down upon warden and miscreant alike.

*   *   *

Almost at once, too, I met the Dean, actually in the shadow of the Porch. Eton, Oxford, and the Welsh Guards, he was not hard to

146

identify. In the cathedral, I later discovered, they call him 'Father Mitchell', a disconcerting usage to one of my purposes, but I certainly could not complain about his authenticity *qua* Dean. With a splendid concern his voice rang out, as we sat there on the beggars' bench watching the citizenry pass by—'Good morning, good morning! Lovely day! What a success yesterday—what *would* we have done without you? Morning Simon! Morning Bert! Morning John! (*John Harvey, you know, our greatest authority on medieval church architecture. . . .*)'

The Dean of Wells is a very busy man indeed. He showed me his diary, and it was chock-a-block—even Thursday, resolutely marked as his day off, was nibbled into by a meeting of the Judge's Lodgings Committee. It seemed more the life of an impresario than a cleric, and this is because a cathedral nowadays is far more than just a shrine, but is partly a social centre, partly a concert hall, partly a tourist attraction, and in the case of Wells, very largely a National Concern. A few years ago it was realized that the west front of Wells Cathedral, incorporating an unrivalled gallery of not very exciting but undeniably medieval statuary, was crumbling away: the consequent appeal, launched by an urbane firm of professional appealers, suddenly made Wells, like Venice, better known for its decay than for its survival, and added a new dimension to the life of the Very Reverend the Dean.

It crossed my mind, indeed, so ubiquitous were the symptoms of restoration, that the cathedral's chief function had become its own repair. The building itself, clouded with scaffolding, tap-taps with the hammers of the masons. One frequently sees the Dean, cassocked and umbrella'd, gazing with solicitous eyes at a leprous evangelist or precarious cornice. Outside the west doors there stands a superannuated Victorian pillarbox, painted bright blue, for the acceptance of contributions, and hardly a week seems to pass without some fund-raising function beneath the bold inverted arches of the nave (themselves a restorative device, for they were hastily erected when, in 1338, the central tower lurched twelve feet out of true).

But no, the Dean reassured me over lunch, the true focus of cathedral life remained the daily services which, however infinitesimal the congregations, are held now as always in the panelled seclusion of the choir. Behind the scenes the immemorial functions of the cathedral continue, each with its titular chief: the Baron of the Exchequer, the Chancellor, the Master of the Fabric, the Communar, the Chief Steward. The Dean still presides over the Quinque Personae of his Chapter. The Priest-Vicars, the Lay-Vicars, the Canons Residentiary, the vergers, the twenty-one choristers—all are there to offer their gifts and energies to the daily affirmation of the faith.

I took him at his word, and went that afternoon to evensong: or rather, like nearly everybody else in sight, I loitered about the interior of the cathedral while evensong proceeded beyond the narrow entrance of the choir—allowing me, from the dimmer recesses of the nave, suggestive glimpses of surplices, shaded lamps, anthem sheets, and musical motions within. It was magical. The rest of the great building lay in hush, haunted only by self-consciously shuffling groups of sightseers, and encapsulated there in their bright-lit chamber, as though in heavenly orbit, the Dean, his canons, the musicians and a handful of devoted worshippers performed their evening ritual. The anthem was S. S. Wesley's 'Thou Wilt Keep Him', among the most lyrical in the repertoire, and it was touching to see how many of the tourists leant in silence against pillars, or paused thoughtfully in their decipherment of epitaphs, as the sweet melody sounded through the half-light.

*   *   *

'Can I go and meet Daddy now?' I heard a voice say from the cathedral shop, near the west door (where Mr John Harvey's work seemed to be selling well). 'He's bound to be down from the loft by now.' He was, the last note of the voluntary having faded away into the Lady Chapel, and presently the Organist and Choirmaster, his wife, his two daughters and I were comfortably before a fire in Vicars' Close, the exquisite double row of fourteenth-century houses which runs away to the north of the Chapter House (and which is the only part of the Wells cathedral precinct properly called the Close). Here was Barchester all right! An Oxford print hung above the fireplace; a cat luxuriated on the hearth; books, musical instruments, edibles and Cinzano were all equally to hand. 'Aren't we lucky?' said the children. 'Don't we live in a lovely place? Isn't this a lovely house? We tidied it all up specially for you!'

It was by no means the only musical house in the neighbourhood, for the cathedral precinct of Wells, if it sometimes suggests show business, and often package tours, sometimes feels like one gigantic conservatoire. Muffled from within the cathedral walls, any hour of the day, one may hear the organ rumbling. Celestial through the open doors come cadences of 'Thou Wilt Keep Him'. From old grey houses around the green sound snatches of string quartet, trombonic arpeggios, or tinkles of Czerny. Hardly has the Organist and Choirmaster finished one performance than he is up there again with his choristers, high in their medieval practice room behind Penniless Porch, rehearsing Wood in C minor for the following day.

If faith is the reason for Wells, music is its most obvious diligence. Wells Cathedral School is one of the three schools in England offering specialist education for musically gifted children, tracing its origins to a song school of the thirteenth century, while the music of the cathedral itself is intensely professional. I much enjoyed this feeling of disinterested technique, so remote from commercial competition or union claim. I saw something truly noble to the spectacle of that daily choral celebration, performed to the last degree of excellence, attended by almost nobody but the celebrants themselves: a practice more generous, more frank, more *English* (I ventured to suppose) than monasticism or meditation—and more acceptable actually, one might think, to the sort of gods I myself cherish, the gods of the stones and the lavender, than to the Christian divinity to whom it has, for a thousand years, uninterruptedly been offered.

Before I left Vicars' Close, the children invited me to write something in their autograph books. Visitors always did, they said. I looked with interest at the previous entries, expecting to find there, as one would in a Barchester book, the names of visiting politicians, magnates, or men of law: but no, they were musicians almost to a scrawl—the composers, the instrumentalists, the teachers who pass in a constant stream these days through the busy precincts of Wells. (When I saw what witty things they had written there, I could think of nothing comparably pithy to say myself, so I drew a couple of pictures of the cathedral instead. 'Thought you said you couldn't draw,' the children kindly said. 'We think you're *jolly good*.')

*   *   *

149

The loyalty essential to the myth of Englishness is of course embodied in Wells in the fabric of the cathedral itself, and the enclosure of grass, garden and old stone that surrounds it. For a millennium there have been people in Wells who have devoted themselves to this structure, and it seemed to me that this corporate possession of the little town, like some grand totem or fetish, must powerfully augment the citizenry's sense of community or comradeship.

In a marvellous clutter of sheds, blueprints, and piles of stone, tucked away behind the cloisters, works the Master-Mason of the cathedral, Mr Bert Wheeler. Everybody in Wells, Town or Close, knows Mr Wheeler. 'You've seen Bert Wheeler?' they used to ask me almost anxiously, lest I might have missed him, and if I quoted his opinion on something, the age of an arch, the angle of a subsidence, all argument was stilled. Mr Wheeler has been associated with Wells Cathedral, first as choirboy, then as mason, since 1933, and there is hardly an inch of the fabric that he has not befriended.

How easy it would be, I thought, to fall in love with such a building, and to spend one's life getting to know it, or more usefully perhaps, keeping it there! In the shadow of such permanence, surely life's transient miseries would pass one by? The Master-Mason smiled enigmatically: he is a very practical man. He first fell victim himself to the enthralment of the cathedral when as a small boy he wriggled through a prohibited aperture somewhere in the masonry and so discovered for himself the infinite complexity of the place. Now he knows it all, its unsuspected corridors and hidden galleries, its vaults and its cloisters, and through his yards and offices pass all the architects, the restorers, the masons, the accountants, the surveyors and the builders' merchants perpetually engaged, as they have been for so many centuries, in maintaining the holy structure. He was like the master-at-arms on a warship, I thought, beneath whose experienced eye the workaday life of the vessel goes on, leaving the men on the bridge above, like those priests and choristers at evensong, free to attend to the navigation.

Then there is the Horologist. The most beloved single artifact in Wells Cathedral, I would say, is the medieval Great Clock in the north transept. It is claimed to possess the oldest working clock-face in Europe: whenever it strikes the hour four little horsemen, whirring round and round, knock each other off their wooden horses with lances, while a dead-pan character called Jack Blandiver, sitting stiffly on his seat high on a wall near by, nods his head, hits one bell with a hammer, and kicks two more with his heels.

Every morning at half past eight or so, if you hang around High Street, you may see Mr Ken Fisher of Fisher's the Clockmakers, on his way to wind this endearing timepiece. His father did it before him, his son will doubtless follow, and never was a labour more beloved. 'There's old Jack', says Mr Fisher affectionately as he unlocks the door to the clock gantry, and looks up at the quaint old figure on the wall: and when you have climbed the narrow winding steps, and emerged on the gallery high above the chancel, looking through the inverted arches to the empty nave beyond, then he opens the big glass doors of the mechanism as one might open a cabinet of treasures.

The works are Victorian, the originals being in the Science Museum at South Kensington, and Mr Fisher admires them enormously. What workmanship! What precision! Look at those cogs! Feel how easily the handle turns! (There are three separate movements to be wound up each morning, with a big iron handle, and Mr Fisher is not averse to his visitors helping with the work.) I caught his mood at once, and found the experience oddly soothing. Everything felt wonderfully *handmade* up there, so rich in old wood and dressed stone, with that elaborate gleaming mechanism slowly ticking, and Mr Fisher in his shirt-sleeves cherishing it, and the beautiful cool space of the cathedral beneath one's feet.

'Wouldn't it be good', I said, 'if *everything* in life felt like this?' 'Ah wouldn't it,' said he, resuming his coat after the exertion of the clock-winding. 'But you have to work for it, you see. It doesn't look after itself! Come here now, look down here'—and he showed me down a little shaft to the circular platform on which the four knights of the Great Clock, relieved from their eternal joust until the next quarter hour, were resting woodenly on their arms. 'Now those fellows down there take a lot of looking after. They break so easily, you see. Well they would, wouldn't they, hitting each other with their lances every quarter of an hour? You can't expect them to last for ever, knocking each other about like that!'

*   *   *

In a curious way, I felt, the cathedral was more the property of the Town than of the Close. Bishops, Deans, and Canons come and go (only three Deans have gone on to be Bishops of Bath and Wells), but the shopkeepers and the businessmen, the farmers, even the traders who bring their vans and stalls to Wells Market every week—these people live all their lives in the presence of the great building, and must feel it to be part of their very selves. Wells has its own magnificent parish church of St. Cuthbert, often mistaken by the tourists for the cathedral itself. It has a substantial landed interest and some thriving small industries. But still every street seems to look, every alley seems to lead, almost every conversation seems somehow to turn, to that ancient presence beyond Penniless Porch.

To discover how jealously Wellensians, as citizens of Wells complicatedly call themselves, regard the affairs of the Close, I went to see the newspaper editor. Like nearly everything in Wells, his office is only a step or two from the cathedral, almost opposite the Star (and just up the road from the King's Head which has been unnervingly metamorphosed into a Chinese restaurant). The paper is shortly to move to more modern premises, but its funny old gimcrack buildings are for the moment in High Street, all ramshackle and disjointed, like the kitchen quarters of some dilapidated mansion. How knowingly, I thought, those Linotypes chattered! What intrigues, vendettas, and innuendoes had found their way through those presses, during the 128 years in which the *Wells Journal* has kept its eye impartially on precinct and market-place!

Ah yes, said the editor wryly. There was never a shortage of gossip in Wells, or controversy either. They were an independent sort, the Wellensians. Why, I should have heard the fuss when the Bishop took to culling the wild duck in his moat by shooting them out of his window! Or when they built those dreadful new canons' houses, all trendy streaked concrete, behind the Old Deanery! Oh, yes, Wellensians often resented the airs of the clergymen Up There: though it was not strictly true that the precinct was walled in defence against the assaults of the townspeople, often enough it felt like it.

The Alderman vehemently agreed—the controversial Alderman, everyone called him, who turned out to be a fiery Welshman, bred by the Parachute Regiment out of the Swansea valleys, whose passionately conservationist views during his period as Mayor had led him into bitter conflict with the cathedral. Vividly he recalled those old affrays for me. Had he not threatened to take the Dean to

court when he chopped down the Mulberry Tree? Did he not lead
the opposition to those frightful canonical houses? Was it not he
who instructed his Council, when the Bishop was late for a civic
function, to take their seats without his Lordship?

The Alderman clearly loves a fight, and I rather wished he was
engaged in one just then, so that I could see the sparks fly for myself.
But no, though he spoke to me movingly of an erroneous new
sewage scheme, all was quiet in Wells just then. There had been a
new Bishop and a new Dean since his day, and most of the local
government functions had been taken away to Shepton Mallet. He
sounded rather disappointed, and so was I; for Barchester is not
Barchester, after all, without a battle on its hands.

*   *   *

Or, for that matter, without a Mrs Proudie. It was when I reached
the Bishopric at last that I felt my pilgrimage had failed. Faith I had
certainly found in Wells, diligence, loyalty, pride: but the sense of
authority, of an established order unbreakable and supreme, which
is essential to the Romantic view of England, is lost with the winds
of social change and historical necessity. In Trollope's allegories
that old discipline was represented if not by the person, at least by
the office of the Bishop, splendidly identified by his accoutrements,
his circumstances and his privileges; but the Anglican Bishop of
tradition, gloriously fortified by material well-being and spiritual
complacency—that grand figure of fancy has long gone the way of
the Empire-builder and the top-hatted Station-Master.

As it happens the Bishop's Palace at Wells is perhaps the most
splendid Bishop's Palace of all. Surrounded by its own moat, its
own castellated walls, its own parkland beyond, it stands on the
edge of Wells, in the flank of the cathedral, looking across green
fields into the depths of Somerset. It is like a fortress, and though the
enormous banqueting hall is now only a picturesque ruin, still the
palace is a terrific spectacle. Duck of many varieties paddle its moat,
and the celebrated flotilla of swans which, for several generations,
rang the bell at the gatehouse for its victuals, has recently been
restocked and retrained for the exercise. The palace itself stands
grandly around its yard, with a huge pillared refectory, and a fine
library, and a private chapel—in which, within living memory, daily
choral services were held for the Bishop, his family, and his servants.

But alas, no majestically awful Mrs Proudie greeted me at the palace door. Nobody greeted me at the main door at all, for the Bishop of Bath and Wells now lives only in the north wing of the structure, the rest being devoted to conferences and other useful activities. Gone are the days when the Bishop and his family ate all alone in splendour in the centre of the vast undercroft, surveyed by a gigantic gilded mitre above the fireplace. Gone are those daily services in the private chapel—nowadays the Bishop prays there alone. Gone is the daunting approach to the episcopal Presence, never to be forgotten by curates of long ago, when after treading the long stately corridors of the palace, through the dark gallery lined with portraits of earlier prelates, they timidly opened the door of the great study to discover his Lordship, against a serried background of theological treaties, tremendously at his labours.

The Bishop himself recalled that vanished consequence for me. Now he and his distinctly un-Proudean wife live more modestly, more sensibly no doubt, more Christianly I suppose, but undeniably less impressively in their nicely done-up wing. His new study, furnished in pale woodwork by the Church Commissioners, is unexpectedly emblazoned, around the tops of its bookcases, with a text not from Leviticus or the Sermon on the Mount, but from King Alfred. His visitors' book, when I signed it, contained on the previous page the signature of Peter O'Toole the actor. His car is a Rover—'such a blessing when you're overtaking on our narrow Somerset roads'. This is a very modern, very functional bishopric.

*   *   *

For here at the core the times have overtaken Barchester. The majesty has left the palace. Crowds of people throng to those conference rooms, taking their cafeteria luncheons on canteen tables in the undercroft (where the gilded mitre looms large as ever, but anomalous). Often the gardens are open to the public, and at any time of day sightseers are to be observed hanging over the gate which, inside the great gatehouse above the moat, inadequately (to my mind) asserts the privacy of the bishopric.

Nobody could represent these changes more persuasively than the present Bishop and his wife, who sit in their modest private corner of the gardens, as a Bishop and his lady should, relishing the green and the grey of it all, the long mellow line of their ancient wall, the sweep of the trees and the droop of the trumpet vine, the Turneresque pile of the ruined banqueting hall, the silent towers of the cathedral beyond. But it is not the same. Atavist that I am, yearning sometimes from the austerity of Wales for some of the gorgeous and heedless assurance that used to characterize our magnificent neighbour—nostalgic in this way for the England I am just old enough to remember, I missed the purple swagger and the swank.

For it was partly the conceit of it, Trollope's hubris of the cloth, that captured our imaginations once—now gone it seems, for better or for worse, as utterly from Barchester as from Simla or Singapore.

Cricket at Oxford

Alan Ross

Pedalling between lectures, spokes throwing off
Sun like Catherine wheels, the damp grass
Bestowing its sweetness from a long way off—
Perhaps the Australians were playing
On a May morning, family saloons
Swaying down the Broad *en route*
For the Parks, the whole city—
It seemed to me then—going about
In a daze. Who won the toss,
Who's batting? And arrived,
Breathless from the Taylorian, pockets stuffed
With indecipherable notes on Baudelaire
Les diverses beautés qui parent ta jeunesse
And Rimbaud, it was to exchange
A *fin de siècle* poetry for the more immediate
Mesmeric magic of the score-card—
Macindoe, Lomas, and hazier behind them
Indelible syllables of those lingering others,
Walford, De Saram, Bosanquet, Pataudi.

All day we would marvel at technique
Exercised, it seemed, for its own sake,
The extending of a tradition, as might
Language be refined: an innings
By McCabe packed with epigrams,
Bradman ruthless as if sacking a city.
'Pick, pack, pock, puck', Joyce's
'Drops of water in a fountain
Falling softly in the brimming bowl.'
Language and stroke play, the honey
Of the bats against trees
Whose green might have been arranged
By Poussin or Claude, grouped just so—
That park-music—connived at
And returned to how often for solace—
A refrain running through the years,
Faintly discernible, whatever the distance.

Malmesbury in Springtime

ELSPETH HUXLEY

'It is a nice town, with a fine situation and a most pleasant place to live in,' wrote William Cobbett in the early 1820s, adding that the people looked well-fed. Could he revisit Malmesbury today his opinion, it is pretty safe to say, would remain unchanged.

Malmesbury has changed, of course, but surprisingly little. However much the works of man may overlay the land, they do not reshape its basic structure. Malmesbury's particular merit lies in the fact that it stands upon a hilltop almost surrounded by the river Avon, together with its tributary the Inglebourne. In former times this loop of water provided a natural defence; today it sets a boundary. From the crest of the hill you can look down over grey, stone-tiled roofs, and through gaps in rows of higgledy-piggledy houses, on to water-meadows fringed by poplars and willows, and across to green pastures beyond. On a fine May morning, flowering lilac leans over ancient walls, glimpses of apple trees loaded with blossom show through gateways, chestnuts lift their candles above uneven rooftops, and orderly rows of young plants pattern carefully tended vegetable plots that slope down to the river. It is a reassuring thought that, in this uncertain world, well-fed Malmesburians have been tilling their rich soil, and eating the produce, for well over a thousand years.

The town is dominated by the remains of its once proud abbey, which stand upon the highest point. Malmesbury's own saint, St. Aldhelm, became the first abbot probably in AD 675, and since then Christian worship has been carried on almost without a break in this great grey abbey towering above the lush green fields of north Wiltshire.

After the dissolution of the monasteries in 1539, much of this complex of buildings was demolished by a cloth-merchant called William Stumpe, who bought it from King Henry VIII for £1,517 15s. 2½d. He set up his looms in the nave of the church, which thus survived to become the parish church, as it is today. Nearby, on the foundations of a lodging built by Abbot William of Colerne in the thirteenth century, he constructed for himself a deep-walled, gabled dwelling perched above the river like a castle above its moat. The steep hillside below it, almost a precipice, was terraced then for vineyards, and the massive vaulted undercroft of the abbot's dwelling was no doubt stocked with Mr Stumpe's Malmesbury wine. (Not to be confused with Malmsey.)

More recent occupants of Abbey House kept guns and fox-hunting kit in this ancient undercroft, now used for gentler purposes. After four and a half centuries of secular use, Abbey House has come back into the hands of a religious Order. In 1970 it was bought by the Deaconess Community of St. Andrew, an Anglican Order whose Sisters care for a number of old folk in the house itself, and participate in parish work outside it. With its lawns and gardens, its tall, deep-foliaged trees and mellowed walls, it appears as an oasis in our world of bustle. Yet the High Street with its supermarket is two minutes' walk away. If one word can be singled out to fit this town, it is continuity. Nearly sixteen centuries ago the Irish monk Maildulph, or Mailduib, built his hermit's cell on this spot where, today, prayers from the servants of the same God are daily given.

Seven mills formerly gristed grain along Malmesbury's stretch of river. That just above Goose Bridge—so-called because geese were driven over it to crop a water-meadow where bowls have now replaced birds—was called Wynyards, and above it rise tiers of little houses in place of vines, a sort of vineyard of houses. Another of these mills, the Postern, lay just below a narrow postern gate in the town wall through which benighted citizens could come and go after the main gates had been closed. This old stone mill, rebuilt in Tudor times, stands cheek by jowl with a red-brick brewery erected in 1865, and both now form part of the Linolite factory, the town's biggest employer of labour. Here are made electric light fittings which are exported to forty countries, as well as providing bunk-side lights for the Royal Navy. The factory workers, mostly women, can, in their tea-breaks, watch cattle grazing just across the river and might even see a kingfisher, if they were very lucky.

Attached to the former brewery is a sort of wooden tower up which grain was hoisted into storage bins on top. Now you find, instead of hoppers full of barley, drawing-boards and blueprints and several skilled designers working on improvements to the firm's products. The present chief designer came with the firm from London when it moved here in 1940, and here he has been ever since. He and his wife have become expert country dancers. So much enthusiasm have they kindled locally that there are few evenings when they do not go forth literally to call the tune in surrounding market towns and villages.

Continuity, and walls—everywhere are grey walls, some crumbling, some in good repair, nearly all with plants growing out of, or tumbling over, the stones. The impression they create is not one of severity, but of gentleness. Outlines are curved, roof-tops set at all angles, little flights of winding steps suddenly appear. Nothing is harsh, rigid, or planned. One is reminded of Rupert Brooke's lines: 'Unkempt about those hedges blows/An English unofficial rose.' There is something very unofficial about Malmesbury. In passages too narrow for large vehicles you can hear the footsteps of an approaching person before you see him. The houses have a secretive air. Those who built them must have valued privacy very highly. Privacy, but not unfriendliness: respect, rather, for the right of others, as well as one's own, to withdraw into a private place or to emerge from it at will. Malmesburians would never take kindly to

158

open-plan houses or to the hedgeless, wall-less gardens of North America, where you cannot see where one family's lawn ends and the next begins.

Winding along more or less parallel with the river, with terraced gardens rising steeply above it, is King's Walk. The king concerned was not, as you might expect, King Athelstan, King Alfred's grandson, after whom so many things are named—a street, a garage, a cinema-cum-bingo hall, a bus service—but a Mr Matthew King, M.P. for Malmesbury between 1554 and 1557. He owned the Postern mill and made this Walk to enable farm carts to reach it. To keep an eye on his mill and weir he built a fine Tudor house, King's House, still occupied, but dilapidated, commanding a view over the valley with a garden sloping down to the river. King's Walk leads into another narrow thoroughfare called Burnivale, by which carts could join the Bristol road—the only route in or out of Malmesbury that does not have to cross one of the town's five bridges.

By St. John's Bridge, at the foot of the High Street, stand almshouses put up in 1597 by the burgesses of the old corporation on the site of a much older building, that of the hospital of the Order of St. John of Jerusalem. Here is the still-surviving entrance to this hospice, dating from the late twelfth century, one of the oldest bits of masonry in the town. How squat and thick-walled were these very old buildings, seeming to grow out of the ground on which they stand. By contrast the nineteenth-century silk mills just across the river look bold, severe, and almost stark. First there was a corn mill on the site, then cloth was woven, then it was turned over to silk and then, after an interval of closure, to the dressing of skins. This enterprise was destroyed by a virus, that of myxomatosis, which killed the rabbits that had provided the pelts. So the owner's son switched to a growth industry—dealing in antiques; and today old furniture fills the mill's three spacious floors once noisy with the clatter of looms. Within living memory a bevy of twenty tailors sat cross-legged on the bare upper floors of a house just off the top of the High Street, sewing suits at cut rates for fashionable London firms. In the garden of this same house is an acacia tree, one of six said to have been planted by Thomas Hobbes, the philosopher, who was born in the town in 1588.

Thus industries, like empires, rise and fall. Another that has fallen is lace-making. In 1976, at a Festival of Flowers held in the abbey,

Mrs Annie Goodfield gave demonstrations of this delicate and highly skilled art. She had learnt it from her grandmother, and had made lace used in the trousseau of the Princess Royal (King George V's daughter) in 1912. For this she was paid six shillings a yard. How long did it take to make a yard? Perhaps two weeks, perhaps more, said Mrs Goodfield. She lives now in a terraced two-bedroomed cottage whose dimensions are so small one is tempted to conclude that our ancestors were a race of midgets. Yet into these little dwellings, scrupulously kept, they packed enormous families—she was one of ten—who became large, or largish, men and women. They drew water from a well in the garden (where they kept a pig) to heat up in a copper, had outdoor privies, lamps, candles, a coal-burning grate. The children were packed like sardines in bed, sometimes two beds, one for girls and one for boys. No room to swing a cat. Yet you meet few old folk who do not say that people were happier then, more contented. Perhaps nostalgia for the past is simply a condition of old age, like arthritis.

The High Street speaks for Malmesbury. Winding uphill in a graceful curve, façades have not changed but behind them change has transformed interiors. All have gardens at the back, some mixed up in a most complicated manner with the old town wall, which crops up in unexpected places. The walls of the houses, made of limestone rubble or of brick, are immensely thick. Many pairs of one-up, one-down cottages have been knocked into one and their hive-like interiors refashioned to meet modern tastes. By and large, the poor have given way to the better-off who have bought the houses and put in fitted kitchens, bathrooms, hi-fi's and other adjuncts to modern living. Some are refugees from the rat race of the cities who have found new niches. One such keeps beehives in the gardens of surrounding villages and makes mead in a disused stable.

The High Street curls up the hill and at the top stands the Market Cross, an octagonal late fifteenth-century structure just outside the abbey precincts built for people to shelter from the rain when coming in to market, or from the sun to keep the butter from melting. To remind peasants' wives of higher matters than the price of eggs, the surmounting lantern is carved with figures of saints and of the Crucifixion. Enormous lorries trying to negotiate a sharp turn into Gloucester Street have knocked bits off the buttresses and there is a constant need for repairs. Beyond the Cross lies the abbey church with its magnificent Norman south porch, one of the finest, it is said, in all England.

The façade of the Old Bell Inn abutting the abbey is smothered, at this time of year, with wisteria blossom, humming with bees. Part of the abbey's original buildings, probably a guest-house, is incorporated into the inn's structure. A guest might find himself in a bedroom with fifteenth-century moulded beams and medieval windows. Should he go for a stroll in the garden at the back, he would come to an octagonal gazebo, dated 1642, approached by steps covered by a white-flowering rock-plant sometimes called snow-in-summer. Thence a long flight of crumbling stone steps winds steeply down to a footbridge crossing the river below a weir which served one of the seven mills.

Had you been looking down from the gazebo thirty years ago, you might have seen a train puffing importantly out of a now vanished station. It would not have been embarking on a long journey, just six miles and four furlongs, bound for Dauntsey where it connected with the London-to-Bristol line. Nor would it have been a large train, just two passenger coaches and a locomotive, known locally as The Bunk. But it had been firmly fixed in the affections of Malmesburians ever since its opening, amid town bands, mayoral send-offs and much rejoicing, in 1877. There were no bands, banners or official mourners at its funeral eighty-five years later when it closed down, killed by road transport. Its drivers and firemen were respected citizens who would hold the train if they saw a late-comer sprinting towards the station, or set down a farmer's wife with her shopping near her gate, or pick up a rabbit caught in a snare. There was an occasion when the driver stopped the train to give his son a lesson in grafting crab-apple trees. The sole porter kept his hens in a run beside the signal-box. Drivers became so devoted to their engines that one, Ted Jones, who served the Great Western Railway for forty-seven years, had the outlines of his puffer carved on his tombstone, where it can be seen in the cemetery a few hundred yards away.

All traces of the line have gone save for one disused engine-shed, and the station yard, with a stretch of level riverside meadow beyond, has been set aside for light industries. Three have so far built small factories, sited as discreetly as possible beside the river. To reach the town, another long flight of steps takes you up past

Abbey House to the Market Cross and the shops beyond. Or, at the top, you may branch off along another of those narrow, high-walled passages to arrive at Holloway, one of the routes out of town. I explored this passage behind a lady who was followed by a collie dog. When we reached the street, the dog rested his front paws on a rail which guarded the passage's exist, thus enabling his owner to fix a lead to his collar without bending down. The dog then took her shopping-bag in his mouth and ambled on ahead of her into Cross Hayes, where the Town Hall—now re-named Civic Centre—stands, and towards the shops beyond. The citizens of Malmesbury have changed, yet not changed, in the eleven centuries that have passed since their town received its Royal Charter. They are still quiet-mannered; reasonably, if not excessively, industrious; fond of gardening, fond of leisure; well-fed; not to be hurried. And they still find Malmesbury to be a nice town, with a fine situation and a pleasant place to live in.

Cambridge in Wartime

JACQUETTA HAWKES

1. *The Child in Autumn*

In Trinity the chestnuts ripen,
Cambridge kindles autumn fire;
My son and I, our baskets bearing,
Go to seek our hearts' desire.

Along the Backs the lawns are sodden,
Willows trail their latter green,
And our gentle, learned river
Dark with wisdom flows between.

On the path each nut is glowing
Warm beside its snowy husk,
So much richness, so much roundness
We could gather day to dusk.

Soon, unleashed, the boy is darting
Here and there with serious face,
While the mother, distant, watching,
Marvels at his heedless grace.

Now these long leaf-nourished gardens
Are peopled softly from the past,
Among the mellow shades the shadows
Linger where their lot was cast.

Bentley, Bacon, Herbert, Housman—
Autumn ghosts are walking there;
Newton's mind pursues the echo
Along its cloistered thoroughfare.

Not for them my heart is beating,
Not for great ones such as these,
But for a small phantom threading
In and out the chestnut trees.

Where the son goes there the mother
Went in autumns sweet as this;
In his laugh her laughter echoes,
In her footsteps follow his.

From the lawns the mist is rising,
Homeward now our steps are bent,
Bearing in our laden baskets
Heart's desire and heart's content.

2. Rooks

Familiar rooks, I wake to hear you calling
And through my window see you rising, falling,
Borne like black ashes on the bonfire's breath;
Old haunting cries that never
Cease, but sound forever
Echoing through life's roof-tree on to death.

Cambridge in Wartime

When I an infant in the garden sun
Lay heedlessly, your same calls must have run
Through my small skull; they interlace
My hours of early dreaming,
And now I see you streaming
In sable lines, far, far before my face.

Rooks, whose unchanging calls remain in tune
With every season. April mounts to June
And autumn bends to winter's low hung skies,
But still your voices' sound
Accompany their round
And with their themes mix, mell and harmonize.

When roused by spring's first stirring sigh
You hasten to bare bough, what promise I
Hear in your babel; leaves will soon be frilling
Your stark and naked nests
Where underneath black breasts
Lie golden-hearted worlds with new life filling.

How could summer support her ardent skies
Without the spanning rafters of your cries?
Which heard above the nearer sound of bees
Bring to the idle shade
On lawns by elm trees laid
Some exaltation of the noonday ease.

Flocking in autumn, then your voices hold
The richness of the ploughland, fold on fold,
Where jet among the gulls you take your fill
Until your cohorts wing
Where the bow of evening
From frail green east to glowing west, is still.

Yet beyond all it is the realm of winter
That is most truly yours, for your notes splinter
The icy air and crackle in the frost,
And when storms are hurling
Your beaten wings go swirling
As on their fans the flying year is tossed.

Familiar rooks, long may I hear you calling
And wake again to see you rising, falling,
All past and future threaded with your weft.
As with the years' swift way
So with my seasons stay
In tune, great birds, nor cease when I have left.

VIEWS OF LONDON

O, towne of townes! patrone and not compare,
London, thou art the flour of Cities all.

WILLIAM DUNBAR, *In Honour of the City of London*

St. Paul's Cathedral, London by John Piper

The East End

PRAFULLA MOHANTI

I lived in a tiny room on the third floor of an old Victorian building in the East End of London. It was in the autumn of 1965 and I had to come to London to work as an architect. My building was situated on busy Commercial Street, near Aldgate East tube station. It was part of a group of decaying buildings around a courtyard used for car parking and children's play. There were no lifts or proper washing facilities. But the buildings, with brick arches and open balconies, had immense charm and a distinct character.

Several families lived there with their children, pets, and possessions. But I was alone and a long way away from my home in a village in eastern India.

I found London a lonely place. I could not understand the British mind. Adapting to a different set of standards and values and making the unknown my own, created tension inside me. There were personal problems which I could not share with anybody.

Self-realization was slow. Finding my identity in an alien culture was painful. But the East End helped me. I walked for hours thinking, looking at life and old buildings. The empty churches provided me with temples for silence and meditation. The river Thames listened patiently to my tales of loneliness. I enjoyed the colourful street markets and watching people eat jellied eels. The slums, the church towers, the river and the docks with long serpentine brick walls, the tramps waiting outside the pubs, had a sense of unity. I thought the East End was a real place with honest and friendly people.

A small man in his forties stood at the bottom of the stairs in the morning. He was quiet and gentle and always wished me good morning. One day I found out that he was a window cleaner and had to work hard to earn his living.

Every night, after the pubs closed, I heard people quarrelling in the room above me. There were shouts and screams and the noise of furniture being smashed. A dog would bark in the next room. I was worried in case somebody was getting hurt. Then suddenly there was silence.

171

One night as I was preparing to go to bed there was a knock on my door. I opened it and was surprised to see the window cleaner. I invited him in.

'I need your advice,' he said. 'I live in the flat above you with my wife and stepson. They don't like me. It's my flat but they treat me as an outsider. So every evening I go to the pub and get drunk. When I return home we have quarrels and fights. What can I do? I feel so miserable. I need love.'

'Don't get drunk,' I said.

From that night I heard no more sound of quarrels.

The incident gave me an insight into British life. I thought people were frank and open when it came to expressing themselves to strangers.

But I didn't want to remain a stranger. I wanted to be involved with life. It was difficult to make spontaneous friendships with adults, so in the evenings I taught the local children to paint and dance. Through them I learned a great deal about life in the East End.

They had no inhibitions in expressing their affection for me. They needed me as much as I needed them, who were neglected by their parents.

Sometimes while walking along the streets I heard voices calling out, 'Sir, sir!' I looked around. There were the children standing on the balconies of tenement houses waving at me. They were like flowers. They gave me a sense of reality.

Brick Lane was safe. There was no sense of violence and I thought Jack the Ripper was only a myth. It was a long street consisting of old buildings occupied by traders of Indian and Jewish origin. The cloth shops were like Aladdin's cave. Once you entered through the narrow doorway you found fabrics of all kinds stored on racks. I bought materials for my canvases there. When the shopkeepers knew I was an artist they were kind and helpful and sold me their old stock at a reduced rate.

There were a couple of Indian restaurants run by men who had left their families behind. One of them was good and reasonably cheap. Often I ate there. The owner, a man in his thirties, with an oily dark skin and a round face, sat at the cash desk keeping account carefully. An Englishwoman in a sari was always there to help him. She was thin, tall, and there was a sign of contentment on her face.

The East End

One evening I was having my meal when three Englishwomen entered the restaurant. Suddenly the atmosphere became tense. Soon they had an argument with the woman in the sari who told them, 'I'm not a whore like you. I'm married. I'm respectable.'

The women thought that was funny and were sarcastic. So she turned to the Indian and asked him to tell them that he had married her.

But he just sat there with a grin on his face.

I saw the Odeon cinema change its name to Naz, showing Hindi and Bengali films. Every night people gathered in front of the cinema and gossiped. The colourful posters and the Indian women in saris gave the place an Eastern flavour.

A little way away, just off Commercial Road, was Hessel Street. It was a beautiful slum and the narrow street was given life and colour by Indian grocers and Jewish butchers. There was an atmosphere of joy and happiness.

But Brick Lane and Hessel Street have now changed. A part of Hessel Street is pulled down while Brick Lane has become more prosperous, with restaurants, grocers, record and sari shops, and travel agents. You can buy everything from the Indian sub-continent, highly-scented cosmetics, spices, mangoes, exotic vegetables and even fish from tropical streams and ponds. Frozen of course. But if you prefer to see them swimming in their clear blue waters you can easily buy a cut-price ticket to Bangladesh or Calcutta from one of the many travel agents.

Brick Lane has acquired a character of its own; with Bengalis strolling along at every street corner, it could very well be a street in Calcutta. The old restaurant has now become famous. It has got a licence to sell beer. I have noticed young English people eating there.

On Sunday mornings the street gets crowded with visitors. Nearby Petticoat Lane comes to life with strange voices from all over the world. Street vendors sell practically everything, transistors from Hong Kong and carving knives from Korea at bargain prices. Young men try to sell copies of the *Socialist Worker*.

Outside Blooms, the famous Jewish restaurant, a long queue of people waits to buy salt beef and latkas. The Whitechapel Art Gallery next door remains nearly empty.

Around midday the traders prepare to leave. The crowd thins out. In the afternoon the streets look like a deserted battlefield.

There was a row of shops right opposite my building. A middle-aged woman ran the bakery. She was kind and friendly. She knew everybody in the area. She was tall, thin, neatly-dressed, and always carried a poodle in her arms. It was like her baby and she put the poodle on a chair as she served the customers. I bought my bread from her.

One day she said, 'Darling, you look so lonely. I live upstairs alone with my poodle. Why don't you come up and see me tonight?'

The woman standing next to me said, 'Oh, she fancies you!'

I promised to see her, but I didn't go.

The next day I went to buy my bread, but she didn't ask me why I hadn't visited her.

My building was scheduled to be pulled down. I moved to another part of the East End, Wapping.

Recently, I went back to my old street. My building was gone. In its place stood a modern lifeless box. Most of the shops were closed down, but the bakery was still there. I went inside. As soon as the woman saw me she recognized me and said, 'Darling, where have you been? I haven't see you for ages.'

Going to live in Wapping was like a dream come true. While living in Aldgate I came visiting often. Walking along cobbled Wapping High Street was an experience in itself. The old deserted warehouses with overhead connecting bridges and the smell from the spice mill created a surrealist atmosphere. I sat on the river bank gazing at pieces of driftwood. I liked the view, the church spires of Rotherhithe and warehouses right on the waterfront. Behind me there was a piece of green grass where children played.

I thought Wapping was romantic. It was like a village. Everybody knew everybody. It was an isolated community of friendly working people, tightly packed into a few blocks of flats surrounded by docks and warehouses. There were more pubs to people than anywhere else I know. Two famous pubs were situated along the river, the Prospect of Whitby and the Town of Ramsgate, both with river views. The Prospect of Whitby was popular among the tourists. The locals rarely visited it and looked at it with suspicion. Coachloads of tourists came every evening. Often one found tourists coming out of Wapping Underground Station wondering which way to turn for the Prospect of Whitby.

City Construction by Paul Brierle

But the Town of Ramsgate had retained its old charm, with a regular clientele. It was situated in the most picturesque part of Wapping with The Pierhead, a group of unified Georgian houses with a magnificent view of the river on one side and Oliver's Wharf on the other. Adjoining it were a beautiful church tower, badly damaged in the war and with shrubs growing on it, a very old school building a man had been converting for many years, and a pretty little park with matured trees and children's playground. The tall wall which enclosed part of the cemetery opposite Oliver's Wharf continued along the street around the park and gave it a unique walled-garden effect.

I enjoyed living in Wapping. I spent long hours watching the river Thames flow gently towards the sea. I saw her changing moods, not only during the day due to high and low tides, but during seasons. The reflection of the pink sky on summer evenings made the river glow with warmth and the rising mist in autumn created an air of melancholy. I saw the river in rain, in snow, and in brilliant sunshine. I watched the raindrops fall on the water and make patterns. I could have spent my whole life just staring at the river.

I walked to various parts of East London and admired the fine churches designed by Nicholas Hawksmoor. The parish church of Spitalfields with steps leading to the portico had an inspiring presence. St. George-in-the-East on The Highway gave the surrounding council flats an identity. Its simple interior reconstructed after the war was peaceful.

Wapping is changing. There is a grand scheme to develop the dock area. Many warehouses have been pulled down and docks filled in with rubble to provide space for housing. St. Katharine's Dock has been transformed into a luxury marina with a characterless modern hotel with wonderful views of the river and Tower Bridge. Oliver's Wharf has been converted into luxury flats and The Pierhead is inhabited by people whom the East Enders consider belong to the West End.

I felt like an intruder in the beginning. My flat was situated on the first floor of a tenement block with entrance from a covered balcony. The buildings, grouped around a central courtyard, looked like a stage set with washing hung on strings, people gossiping, and single old people standing alone on their balconies, looking down silently and observing life. The children played everywhere, smashing milk bottles.

I felt sorry for the children whose parents were not interested in them. I tried to teach at the Youth Centre but found it impossible. The children were not interested in art. The glass windows of the Centre were always smashed and boarded up.

The evenings were dull for the young people in Wapping. So they gathered at street corners looking for excitement.

An old man lived in a bed-sitter on my floor. He was sick and looked sad. Soon we became friends and he told me all about his life and family.

On the ground floor lived an old woman. She was confused but very beautiful with well-kept curly white hair. Often she came out of the flat wondering where she was and her daughter quickly took her inside again.

A few yards away a very old lady sat by her window watching people pass by. She looked fragile and as soon as she saw me she drew the curtains and hid her sensitive little face. I discovered that she was the oldest surviving member of the community and had a very large family.

One afternoon black limousines arrived in the courtyard covered with elaborate wreaths. The old lady had died.

It was an autumn night in 1974. I was returning home after spending a happy evening with friends in Chelsea. A group of young people followed me from Wapping Underground Station along the deserted streets shouting 'Pakis and Indians stink of curries.' As I was about to enter my building I was attacked and left lying unconscious in the middle of the courtyard. When I woke up it was like getting up from a beautiful sleep. I was sad that it was broken.

But my romance with the East End vanished.

When I first came to England I did not know there was a place called the East End. I will always remember it. It has played an important part in my development not only as an artist and writer, but also as a person. It has provided me with love and hate and the solitude and isolation essential for my work. I have lived and suffered in my own world of dreams surrounded by a real world of slums, squalor, violence and honest human beings. I watched the beautiful buildings, old squares and streets being pulled down. I wanted to scream 'Stop!' Soon large skyscrapers stood there, monuments to the municipal authorities and their brilliant architects. The old slums were soon replaced by new slums.

But still the river continues to flow, the bushes grow on old railway arches and I have seen them blossom.

Members of the Garden

ALETHEA HAYTER

For centuries it was a graveyard. Now it is a public garden, of a kind. The roofless shell of the bombed church shuts it off from the raucous City street beyond, and it is a quiet and almost secret hollow among the cliffs of office blocks. It is not much frequented by ordinary citizens. Typists sometimes eat their sandwiches here at lunch-time, but for the rest of the day it becomes once more the domain of its real inhabitants. They regard the benches as theirs; they will not seem to notice you if you go and sit there, but you will be made to feel an intruder—unless you yourself are beginning to be one of them.

The paths are paved with old tombstones, so defaced by passing feet that only snatches of their original inscriptions—'who departed this life . . .', '. . . of the 9th Regiment of Foot', '. . . are deposited the remains . . .'—can still be made out. Other tombstones have been moved and replanted round the edge of the garden, and on them one can make out some longer sentences: 'This monument was erected by his Sorrowful Widow', 'Upwards of twenty years Assistant Sexton of this Parish'. An occasional physician or admiral is commemorated, but more often it is a 'Merchant and Citizen of London' who dimly signals to posterity through the lichen. The Christian names on the tombstones are mostly the serviceable and perennial ones—George, Richard and Thomas, Alice, Susannah and Mary Ann—but by peering and poking one could compile an anthology of pleasant names now half-forgotten: Saul and Euphemia, Rowland and Clemency, Nathaniel and Jacobine, Theophilus and Tryphena, Joshua, Jabez, Matilda,

Richenda and Sybella. Near the centre of the garden there is a table-tomb which has not been moved like the others. It is cracked and flaking, and part of the inscription has blurred away, but if you press your face against the iron railings round the tomb, you can just make out

ALSO OF

DAME ANSTICE PR . . .

RELICT OF THE ABOVE

BORN 16TH DECEM . . .

The rest is under the strangling stems of bindweed which has spread its flaccid white parachute flowers and shield-shaped leaves around the base of the tomb and all up one end. What would Dame Anstice's husband, that erstwhile City dignitary, have thought if he could have known that her name, but not his, would be visible to the passer-by three hundred years later? Was it typical of their married life? Was Dame Anstice a tartar?

It is not much of a garden, perhaps. There are two robust plane trees and one sycamore, but the lilac bush in the north-east corner, which never gets any sun, looks limp and discouraged compared with the buxom fruition of the stone pineapple finial from the roof of the bombed church, which lies under the bush. Two months ago the laburnum which droops over one of the benches must have been covered with strident yellow; now it only dangles with dun and poisonous pods. Floribunda roses have been planted in the two narrow flower-beds, but they look leggy and inappropriate. The modest sturdy wild flowers which poke out between the railings of Dame Anstice's tomb are more at home here. They are all in the July colours—the yellow of ragwort and mustard and groundsel and of the fat hearts of white-frilled yarrow, the purple of willow-herb and of the five-petalled mallow with its mauve and plum stripes like a circus tent. Nearest to glory are the rich honey-smelling amethyst plumes of the buddleia which crowds behind a stone sarcophagus with pricked terrier ears at each corner.

The pigeons and sparrows do not bother with the groundsel. They grow fat on the crumbs dropped from the typists' sandwiches, and they have still more reliable friends, who come here to feed them. The old woman on the end bench, who is wearing a stained mackintosh over a tweed coat, and has her hat tied down with a

179

woollen scarf, although it is a stuffy July afternoon, has a paper bag out of which she is bringing whole handfuls of crusts, and the pigeons are jostling round her feet to snatch at the bread as she lets it dribble from her arthritic fingers.

The pigeons, with their coral feet and gold-rimmed eyes, their iridescent necks and sophisticated grey and white stripes and flounces, ought to be as elegant and admired for their colour scheme as jays or pheasants, but they are too fat, they have let their figures go, and are flabby and dishevelled like slum landladies; you never seem to see them preening themselves. A few flaps of their wings from here, and they can be in Trafalgar Square where besotted tourists will gorge them with corn as they condescendingly sag down on to outstretched arms to be photographed. They are layabouts who do not have to earn their living, nor to keep up appearances. But the woman with the paper bag of crusts likes them, and likes the quick impertinent sparrows in their dingy black and brown suits. She likes them better than human beings.

The men and women who are the true inhabitants of this garden are all solitaries. They are not all old, nor are they all poor. They are not homeless; presently they will go back to some dark and cluttered room to sleep. It is rare to see a tramp here, and very rare to see a real drunk, flat out on a bench sleeping it off with an empty bottle on the ground beside him, or a staring junkie. The place, and its real owners, can make that sort of outsider uncomfortable and send him shambling off. The people who sit here all afternoon never say a word to anyone else, though sometimes they talk to themselves. They are shabby but not ragged. The women have thick wrinkled stockings, and clutch half a dozen limp carrier bags. They do not care in the least what other people think of them. They do not see other people at all. Each has a private world, closed and entire, in which other people are not wanted.

The garden is a peaceful place because its inhabitants are solitary without being lonely. They are London's hermits, to be carefully distinguished from London's witches, the haters of other people's happiness, the mutterers and quiet snarlers who feel threatened and persecuted by the very existence of other people, and who protect themselves by believing that their ill wishes can follow those other threatening existences home, and squirm under their pillows at night. My first meeting with a London witch was on a fine sunny morning forty years ago when, as I was walking along a Westminster street, pleased with life and myself, a woman who was passing—a respectable-looking middle-aged woman whom I had never seen before, neatly dressed in brown, with the appearance of a trusted housekeeper—suddenly turned on me and said, 'You'll never do well, you six feet of misery. I could kill you if I liked.'

I was twenty years younger, and a head taller, than she was; yet she was certain she could kill me. She cannot have thought she could attack me then and there in the street. No, she was going to go home and make a wax model of me, and stick pins into it and melt it by the fire—why, who knows, for I was a perfect stranger to her. I must have insulted and attacked her by being happy. Since then I have seen other London witches, in buses, at street corners, with a confident power of hatred in their eyes as they watched groups of young laughers, and wished them ill.

Such witches may occasionally stray into the garden, and fidget restlessly on a bench for a short time, but they are not true members of the garden. The real inhabitants are beyond the reach and threat of other present-day good fortunes and existences. They are truly alone in their worlds, and happy there. The man by Dame Anstice's tomb has a torn manilla envelope full of dog-eared papers which he takes out and reads over and over again. His lips are pursed into a smile; he is reliving past victories over shadowy bureaucrats, past triumphs of successful repartee and scoring-off. The woman feeding the birds is even further enclosed in her world; there are no human beings, even shadowy ones from the past, in it, only the careless, greedy, self-absorbed pigeons. She and they are free.

Her paper bag of crusts is empty, and presently the pigeons and sparrows move off. The smeary mother-of-pearl of the sky above the sycamore is thinning towards the pale yellow transparence of late afternoon, and there is a small stir of air in the garden, just enough to float the spicy smell of the buddleia a little way among the tombstones. There is a rustle in the lilac bush, and a blackbird looks out. The old woman, avoiding any sudden movement, puts a hand carefully into her pocket and brings out one more crust, which she drops near her feet. The blackbird makes some tentative hops which bring him within a yard of the crust, but he cannot quite decide whether to risk that last yard. Then it is too late; hovering and whirring like inquisitive little helicopters, the sparrows are back and have got in first and carried off the crust. The old woman watches but does not interfere.

I sat for a time in the garden the other day. I had been shopping, and was laden with plastic bags; certainly I was untidy, and it is quite likely that my stockings were wrinkled; my lips may have been moving as I turned over on my tongue some *mot juste* which I had just found for the chapter I was in the middle of writing. After a quarter of an hour's rest and reverie, I looked up suddenly, and saw that two passing girls were staring and giggling at me. They had recognized an incipient Member of the Garden.

As the War Left It

Mark Girouard

During my first autumn at preparatory school a row of bushes along one side of the roller-skating rink became the scene of one of the school's periodic crazes. This time it was for caves or houses. Like insects we wormed our way into the undergrowth and made secret hides for ourselves, lined and made snug with dead leaves and swathes of hay. We each had our house, and only our best friends were allowed inside them.

My own hide took its place in a long line of secret places, stretching far back into childhood—caves under tables or behind sofas, abandoned cupboards, secret lofts over false ceilings, hollow trees, labyrinthine tunnels inside the thick pine-scented foliage of wellingtonias. Some of these were my personal preserves, some shared with my sisters or cousins. Later on at school, I began to become more ambitious and to extend my territory. On the steep hillside a little above the school was a field abandoned to bracken, with a plantation of pines above it. In high summer the bracken grew well above my head and became a secret world, threaded by my own personal tunnels. Hidden in the bracken were wild or abandoned raspberry bushes, half smothered but still giving fruit; a clearing in the plantation was thick with wild strawberries. About a mile from the school was another large area of abandoned hillside, known as the Hag. It was scrub-covered and stony, and there was a disused quarry at the top of it. Violets and primroses flowered on the Hag before anywhere else; rare oxslips grew in the quarry; and later in the year spikes of Aaron's Rod towered out of the hillside, like huge yellow foxgloves half covered with grey fur.

I had proprietorial feelings about both these places. No one disputed them; I once came across a man setting snares on the Hag, but he was the only other person I ever met there. I sometimes shared the Hag with a friend, but kept the bracken and raspberry field to myself.

I suppose the contrast to the communal life of classrooms, dormitories, ink-stained desks, iron beds, and bare bulbs made these private kingdoms especially attractive to me. At any rate, the habit of appropriation remained with me all through my schooldays and long after them. Moreover, England in the years after the war was full of lonely places. There was no need to go into the country to find them. The oddest ones were in the cities.

At Oxford it was the area around the gasworks that especially attracted me. It was impossible to feel any sense of personal possession about the historic parts of Oxford; one could sense, over all its beautiful or ancient buildings, the thick invisible film of all the eyes that had been admiring them. But the gasworks area seemed to belong to me almost as much as my own dreams. It was possession I wanted, not understanding; I knew nothing about the making of gas, or the lives of the people who lived in the little houses. Knowledge would have spoilt the dreamlike quality of the two-storey terraces, built of a chequerwork of red and white bricks, and the long narrow streets which always seemed to be empty. On occasions I and some friends penetrated into the gasworks themselves at night and found another unreal world of silent shadowy figures silhouetted in front of the red glow of furnaces. The Thames ran past the gasworks; and something about the process of gas-making attracted the swans, who were always there in far greater quantities than in cleaner and more obviously picturesque reaches of the river.

London as the war left it, and as it lingered on until the property boom shattered its peculiar quality, was full of places empty enough for one or two people to feel that they owned them. Hugest and oddest of all was the great waste left by the Blitz to the north of St. Paul's. This lives in my memory as deserted and peaceful as the Campagna must once have been—except that it was pink willow-herb that covered it, rather than sun-bleached grass, and instead of Roman ruins the shattered remains of Wren churches and Victorian office-blocks rose up through the undergrowth. A climb down from the pavement to what had been basement level led to a long lonely walk through the ruins. In the middle of the devastation, miraculously untouched, was a small building, little more than a cottage, with a lean-to adjoining. If one rang its bell, and was lucky, a friendly caretaker appeared and opened up the lean-to. Inside, glittering in the shadows, was the enormous bulk of the Lord Mayor's coach.

The St. Pancras Hotel was another curious place. It had long ceased to be a hotel. There were offices down below, and rooms for railway staff on the top two or three floors; but a good deal of it was just empty. The best time to visit it was on Sunday morning, when the offices were closed and whoever occupied the upper floors seemed to be either asleep or away. The main entrance was shut on Sundays, but there was a side entrance letting on to the station concourse. This was always open, and usually unguarded.

The wild skyline of the St. Pancras Hotel was common property, but in the 1950s the interior was completely unknown. When I first walked into the great staircase it was like discovering a cathedral which no one had ever heard of. I can still remember the total silence in which I walked up the huge curving flights of stairs, where the soot-covered carpet absorbed all sound—up past arcades of gothic columns and arches, up past a painted alcove, where grimy medieval lovers courted their mistresses, up and still up until the stairs ended beneath a roof vaulted like a cathedral, and painted with stars.

A suite of dirty and empty rooms on an upper floor led to a window, and the window led to a catwalk which stretched into the distance across the vast ballooning roof of the train shed. Broken or open panes here and there gave views of toy trains and tiny people far below. Even more exciting was the route up through the entrails of the cloche-shaped roof of the main tower to the ten-foot square platform at the top. Access to the inside of the roof was by way of a ladder and trap-door on an upper landing. Above this was a vast

184

cave, tangled and criss-crossed overhead with a network of timber that loomed dimly out of the twilight. More ladders climbed and shook perilously up through the timbers to a second trap-door, which gave on to the flattened apex of the roof.

The Caledonian Market in north London was not as dramatic as St. Pancras, but in its way it was even stranger. It had been built as a sheep and cattle market in the 1850s. Everything had been carried out on the grandest scale. The market square was the size of a parade-ground, and out of the middle a clock-tower rose like a campanile from a piazza—or a lighthouse from an abandoned headland, for financially the market had been a disaster. At each of the four corners was an identical and very large public house. In the middle of one side were two large hotels, also identical. Pubs and hotels were designed like Italian palaces, in the clubhouse taste of their time. By the post-war years two of the pubs were derelict, and the hotels had become tenements. A small corner of the market was used by the Post Office, but otherwise it was empty. All round the market long empty roads were lined by rusting but splendid iron railings, surmounted at intervals by cast-iron sheep's heads. At the end of each vista a pub stood up like a lonely tower. The market itself was a desert of grass and thistles. The best time to visit it was at night, when a cool breeze rustled the thistles, and the clock-tower stood out against the stars.

Yet for night-time walking there was nothing to equal the docks. Even by daylight the narrow canyons sunk between cliffs of warehouses that followed the curve of the river through Wapping, Bermondsey, and Rotherhithe were strange enough. At night, dimly lit by occasional lamps, they were sensational. The streets were completely enclosed; nothing but the brick walls of warehouses to either side, and high overhead the occasional thin line of an iron bridge joining building to building. But every now and then a slit of passage went down to the river. One of these, at Cherry Garden Pier, led to a wooden causeway, and the causeway led to a floating wharf in the river. From here one could look out across the whole width and curve of the view to the silhouette of Tower Bridge, and be alone with the gurgle of the water as the tide ran out, and the melancholy booming of the moored barges as they knocked against their neighbours.

The last time I visited Bermondsey, rows of warehouses were

standing empty, with their doors swinging open and the streets thick with rubbish. Demolition wasn't long away. Some of the places I used to visit remain, more of them have disappeared, all of them have changed.

Hampstead Heath

JOHN HILLABY

Almost everything happened that morning. Cuckoos were calling. Two Holly Blue butterflies danced like mad over a patch of muddy water. You could hear the frogs nearly half a mile away. A vulgar noise that might be likened to someone belching into a microphone. I discovered a glory of flowers, the most beautiful, the most surprising I have ever seen on the Heath. A Zoroastrian touched my forehead with his ring. But let's start on a quiet note and keep what's left of the surprise to the end.

About thirty years ago, a number of us, all naturalists, blocked the ditch laid down to drain West Meadow which lies immediately to the south-west of the great lawns of Kenwood House. And lo!—as they used to say—from the resultant bog that covered up our deviation from rectitude, there emerged some very interesting plants including insect-catching sundews, horsetails, several liverworts, and rare mosses. The place is now called an S.S.S.I., a Site of Special Scientific Interest. A year, or maybe two years later, I wandered down there to see what was coming up. Hidden away among the rushes and sedge was not one but several spikes of Early Purple orchids, nicely accommodated in slightly acid clay soil. A glorious sight. I went down on my knees to pluck the portion of a flower and a spotted leaf for identification purposes and partly covered over the plants to keep them from uncharitable eyes. I recall looking up at the sky, the better to straighten my back. But soft—as they also used to say—I was observed.

A man stood on the path with his arms folded. A striking-looking man. Golden skin. A slightly Armenoid nose. In fact, in profile, not unlike Conrad Veidt who, incidentally, once lived in West Hampstead. But it wasn't him. With a courteous bow, he asked if I were of their faith. 'What faith?' I enquired. Before answering he held out his ring of sky-blue lapis lazuli, curiously carved. 'A Zoroastrian,' he said. If I remember rightly he was the head of the British community and thought from my posture that I, too, worshipped the sun which, of course, I do, though more from pragmatic than mystical reasons. There is no space here to recall what he told me about Ahura Mazda, the Wise Lord, nor of Angra Mainyu who is up to no good at all. But we were in accord under that benign sun and talked for half an hour. Unfortunately I never saw him again. Nor the orchids, for when I returned to the meadow after a short trip abroad they had been grubbed out, roots and all, and may Angra Mainyu curse whoever did it.

The Heath provides constant surprises. Take that as you will. My task here is to give some impression in broad brushstrokes of one of the most famous open spaces in the country for those who don't know it too well, or for thoroughly deprived souls who know it only by reputation. Those frogs, for instance, were not the common kind, but the very noisy edible species, *Rana esculenta* which vent something close to a Gargantuan fart. Aristophanes caught it nicely in that famous line from the chorus which goes something like: *Brek-kek-kek-korax*. It seems that some enquiring herpetologist—or maybe a restaurateur in Heath Street—tipped a pint of spawn from Romney Marshes into the fertile depths of the Red Arches or Viaduct pond where, within a season, a population explosion occurred. In thousands they spread to the women's swimming-pool and then, like my gentle friend and the orchids, were seen no more. There's a Ph.D. in this, but let's keep to generalities.

Today the irregularly shaped Heath, roughly a mile from north to south and a mile and a half from east to west (let's say 800 acres in all), is bigger than Regent's Park but not quite so big as Hyde Park and Kensington Gardens combined. It lies on top of hundreds of feet of clay with here and there a capping of Bagshot sand and glacial pebbles and down-wash. It is a mixture of woodland, scrub, and rough grazing, part of which is used as playing fields. Six ponds give character to the Highgate side and three lie to the south, that is close to Hamstead Heath station on the railway line to Richmond. There are more than half a dozen others which are difficult to describe briefly. Enough to say that water collects on the interface of the porous sand and impermeable clay and emerges as springs or brooklets, some of them iron-stained, which are the sources of three tributaries of the Thames: the Westbourne, the Brent, and the Fleet. Although of little or no medicinal value it was these springs combined with the relatively high altitude, the fresh air, the splendid views, and the rolling ups and downs of the Heath that brought both fame and infamy to Hampstead which became a spa at the beginning of the eighteenth century. Corruption crept in with its popularity and at various periods the streets around the springs and wells were remarkable more for their brothels, gin mills and gambling dens than for quiet recreation. Nor were the land-grabbers slow in seizing widespread opportunities. In 1860 or thereabouts the Heath had shrunk to about a third of its present size.

Let's assume you are taking your cousins from Arkansas, Aberdeen, or Adelaide out on the Heath for the first time and want to show them all that can be easily seen in a couple of hours. You start, I suggest, at Whitestone Pond, clearly an artefact. Don't be deterred by the noise and the whirlabout traffic. Tell them it's *the* highest point in London (440 feet above sea-level) and that Dickens and heaven knows who else lodged in the adjacent pub, Jack Straw's Castle. (Do some homework on Little Dorrit and Mr Merdle.) Cross the road to where the chap sells Sunday papers in the bus shelter and look down first on the crudely cleared scrub that used to attract and sustain charms of goldfinches; second the Vale of Health, and third whatever you can recognize in the Great Wen far below.

Continue with the sun on your right shoulder or back, but not *along* the race-track of the Spaniards Road to the tavern of that name. Keep to the paths almost immediately below it, paths that show clearly how much sand was dug out thereabouts for protective sandbags in two World Wars. If you are on the south-eastern side of the road and don't know how to slip round the back of the Elms, return to the road, drop down the hill and enter the first gate to Kenwood House where booklets will help to fill voids in your local knowledge.

With your back to the southern front of that now blanched and curiously two-dimensional looking home of Boswell's patron, the first Lord Mansfield, spare a tear for Robert Adam. The Ionic pilasters and plastic swags are lost in the almost unicoloured façade. But the interior is lovely, and the view across the lawns and the lakes superb though marred by the dreadful gaps in the profile of the wood, an arboreal slum for which those responsible at County Hall should be boiled in oil and boiled slowly.

At this point in your perambulation you can either turn half left and walk round the eastern flank of the wood until you can see the series of Highgate ponds; or turn right through the self-evident Lime Walk and, among much else, look at the meadow I talked about in my first paragraph. You can't get lost, at least not for long if you keep south, walking mostly downhill, towards the City below. I have missed out much that has fascinated me for years: the extremely old oaks that sprang from the acorns of the ancient Forest of Middlesex; the songful migrants that use the Heath as a kind of aircraft-carrier in a metropolis not otherwise remarkable for undisturbed landing places; the ebb and flow of about 250 different kinds of plants including another orchid, the Lesser Twayblade, that might still survive in Kenwood. The most intriguing question of all is how the place got to be the way it is, a question seldom thought about by local busybodies who think they can put the biological clock back by hacking down trees to 'improve' the view.

I have just space enough to tell you about something which has just seeped into the scientific literature. According to Dr D. Q. Bowen of the University College of Wales, the ancestral Thames flowed around Rothamsted and Bishop's Stortford and reached the North Sea somewhere near Ipswich. That was two million years ago. Down came the first of at least twenty periods of glaciation. One wall of ice reached Finchley. The old Thames was blocked. It rose like a fast-filling bath and may have lapped the Heath. When the ice melted, down poured billions of tons of glacial pebbles of the kind you can pick up on Sandy Heath. Thereafter and at different times around Parliament Hill you might have encountered turtles, reindeer, bears, woolly mammoths, sabre-toothed cats, elks, and lemmings. And throughout that long period the pine forests gave way to mixed forests which, not once but several times, were swamped by steppe and arctic conditions. The Heath was once characterized by heather-clad hills, and not so long ago at that. But no longer and, within this climatic cycle, never again. But what you may discover for yourself is that the Heath is still a glorious place.

PERSONAL
MAP REFERENCE

Had I a song
I would sing it here.

IVOR GURNEY

Cader Idris, Gwynedd by John Piper

England in the Summer

Elizabeth Jennings

Sweetly England stands
In a twilight of rest, of getting ready for sleep.
The sun has left its crimson strands
Over the Western sky. The barley's deep
And gold. England's summer is not like other lands'.

I who love Italy
Can still be caught with emotions offguard when I
Feel England's summons. Harvest will be
Good after tardy Summer. In July
It was rich with Spring but now the Summer is sky

And meadows and woods. The grass
And wild flowers deck the Summer lanes. All this
Was when I felt my childhood pass.
I was one with the rivers' energies.
I plucked the clouds and all the patterned stars.

Love enriched the scene
Of apples and roses. Love chose the season well.
The memory of early love has been
Only happiness here. There sounds a bell.
I weep, I am rich with all this season can mean.

Ploughing Old Furrows with New Eyes

EDWARD STOREY

I wish I had known the poetry of John Clare when I was ten, or fifteen, or even at twenty, for I know of no other poet who teaches us how to *see* the world in which we live and grow.

I had, admittedly, just discovered the poetry of Clare by the time I was twenty, but it has taken another twenty years or more fully to appreciate his individual gift of 'making a miracle out of the ordinary'. And now I am even more excited by his remarkable ability to focus *my* vision on the particular, making me see the familiar as if for the first time.

Clare had a poet's eye long before he began scribbling his poems on the backs of his mother's grocery bags. Perhaps we all have a 'poet's eye' as children but lose it as we grow older and become influenced by what other people see, or expect us to see. Clare never lost the child's fresh view of the world in which he lived, and I needed his writings to remind myself of the many wonders I had seen as a child—wonders I took for granted and nearly buried forever in that dark pyramid of the memory, where they might have mummified or decayed.

Clare grew up in Helpston, in that northern corner of Northamptonshire, an area rich in woodlands and wild flowers. At a crucial period of his life, when he was thirty-nine and almost forgotten, he moved three miles east into the lower, flatter, bleaker landscape on the edge of the Lincolnshire fens.

I was brought up in the western half of the Cambridgeshire fens, only a few miles from Clare's country, and know the villages and walks he wrote about as more than places on a map. I now live in a cathedral's precincts on an invisible boundary between the present and the past, poised conveniently between two worlds.

It is, however, the safer world and landscape of my childhood to which I return again and again for my own writing. As a child I assumed that all the world was as flat, spacious, huge and bright as the world at the end of our street. I had never seen a mountain and probably did not know such things existed. No patchwork-coloured globe spinning in the crowded classroom of my primary school could convince me that the earth was round. Experience taught me otherwise. Day and night there was the land and the sky—two generous opposites. You saw the sun rise from the eastern horizon and move like mercury up heaven's wall until at midday it shone above your head. Then you watched it slide down to the western horizon as the temperature dropped, and it was night again. It was as simple as that. You did not need geography lessons to teach you about the shape of the earth. If there were mountains, forests, cities, lakes and jungles, they belonged to another world that was not my world. My world was flat, big, warm, solitary and almost treeless. It was a world of space and light. It belonged to the wind and skylark, to the heron and reed-mace, pea-fields and harvest, dandelions and poppies—and, of course, childhood.

In those innocent days of discovering that I belonged to such a world I knew nothing of the floods, drainage, riots, resentment and hunger that had made the fen country a bitter place in which to live. I knew nothing of the iron winters that locked the land in a grip of frost and snow making men idle for weeks at a time without work or money. I lived through such times with my family but, as a child, forgot. I knew only of those summers where wheat ripened to mahogany brown; where frayed tassels of barley rustled like silk or moved like shoals of shrimps over the low-tide fields; where harvesters came with clumsy machines to cut and stook the crops, leaving their wigwams of sheaves to dry under an Apache sun. A few days later, when the harvest had been ceremoniously carted home, we were allowed into the fields for gleaning. Towards evening I would pretend to have an abundance of energy just to stay out there long enough to see the cart-wheel moon rise out of that mysterious space beyond the horizon. To see a full moon rising over the fens on any night of the year is to watch a spectacle that must have struck awe into our first fathers. It arrives like a god from secret waters. It rides on the mist and ascends into the sky and, at harvest time, displays its ancient majesty so that even now, with the knowledge that men have walked there, it still makes my spine tingle. As a child my eyes glowed wide with wonder and I went home believing that I had witnessed a divine happening. Although I assumed that everyone on earth shared a similar landscape, with their own vast sky, I believed that only a chosen few were allowed to stay out late enough to watch the arrival of a full moon.

Personal Map Reference

Night has always been a fascination, especially if it is star-lit. The expanse of sky enjoyed during the day is still there when dark but pinned now with a million stars. To stand on a river-bank, away from town, and to look up at the sky's extravagance, is an excitement worth going miles to experience. Stand for a few moments. Forget who you are, and where. Then listen. The fields have taken on a deeper stillness. The only sound might be of sheep snatching at grass, or an owl talking to itself in a willow tree. Slowly you feel yourself becoming part of the night. Your feet strike roots into the soil. Your head reaches towards the stars. The blood beats with a very ancient rhythm as the heart hears echoes too distant to record. I would not want the world round, or crowded with cities at such a time. I listen for forgotten voices, for the dark music that must have trembled over these fens from shadowy faces a thousand years ago.

But, you may be asking, what has all this got to do with John Clare? Simply this, that I needed him to show me what a minute-by-minute thrill of a world it was in which I lived; that everything was significant if only I used my eyes to *see*, to focus closely on the small things as well as the large, and to respect their own timeless history. Clare had a great reverence for life and he taught me how to celebrate. So, although I have always lived within a seven-mile radius of where I was born, I feel now that I have a world full of miracles on my doorstep because each day is re-created with a thousand secrets to discover. Everything I once took for granted I now look at with new eyes. Old furrows are newly ploughed. Skylarks have just been given a new song. The heron is trying out his heavy wings for the first time, and the sky's pattern of clouds has never once been repeated since the earth was made—flat or round.

I even needed Clare to make me see the sky. Throughout his work he refers to it over three hundred times. He describes it as an 'exhaustless sky'; an 'unfrequented sky'; a 'cloud-betravelled sky' and a 'tender-watching sky'. It is also a 'troubled'—'mackerel'—'miser' sky and, when summer goes we are left with 'the desert of a winter sky'. No one has written better about these fenland spaces where 'black clouds mimicked mountains' and the landscape 'spreads from the eye its circle far away'. He frequently referred to the clouds as mountains—they're the only ones we'll have: 'The sun those mornings used to find/Its clouds were other-country mountains . . .'. On other days he tells us how 'the crampt

198

Buriton, Hampshire by Dick Jo

horizon now leans on the ground' or that 'The arch of light around us bowed/Stretches for days its cloudless sky/Save freckling shadows of a cloud/That lose to nothing passing by.'

Slowly I discovered that Clare was describing my landscape in his own individual and unforgettable way, and that if I could train my imagination to see through a similar eye I would find myself looking at a different world each day. When he wrote 'the sheep unfolded with the rising sun' or the heron 'flaps his melancholy wing'; when he described the cart-rut 'rippled with the burden of the rain' or spoke of dandelions that 'closed like painters' brushes when even was', he was talking to me about things I had seen hundreds of times but never with such sharp vision or imagination. So I began to look more closely, to particularize and employ metaphor. I tried to become part of creation, giving names to things that needed renaming. Every season, every day and every hour became important and I began to understand what it meant to be a 'writer of place', to have not only roots in the soil but eyes in my fingertips. I began not only to *see* but to *feel*, to respond with my whole being to wherever I happened to be, and I decided that the people and places I had known all my life were to be the subjects of my books. I had to reappraise the land of my fathers and make it mine. I had to re-enter the child's private world and give it identity. Fortunately, at the age of nineteen, I realized this could be done through poetry, especially when I discovered a year later that John Clare had shown the way. I have carried this belief into my prose—the topography and local history.

When I first visited Clare's birthplace the street still had its village pump and the nightingales still built their nests in Royce Wood. Now they have gone, with many other favourite places he wrote about. I remember it was an early spring day and the sky was overcast. I went with a friend and we picked a few primroses to place at the foot of the poet's grave, then overgrown with long grass and in need of a clean. Afterwards we sat in the church for a while and later walked to the flour mill at Maxey, then on to Glinton and Northborough. Mary Joyce and Patty Clare became as real as the poet himself. The daisies we trod on, the larks above our heads, the grasshoppers and sheep were all direct descendants of the ones he'd celebrated. And, although ugly pylons and railway tracks now disfigured his countryside, the sky and the clouds, the fens' 'faint shadow of immensity', that 'arch of light around us bowed', were just as he had seen them over a hundred years ago. From that moment I believed we had a relationship. It was not idol-worship—we have cursed each other too often for it to be that—but we became neighbours and I, for one, was glad to compare notes and listen to his voice. If Clare found his Eden in the gentler rises of Northamptonshire on the edge of the fens, before Enclosure came to change his world, so I found my Eden in the open spaces of the Cambridgeshire fens before mechanization and urban sprawl changed my world.

After recurring illnesses in infancy I remember my mother taking me for walks in the afternoon—they were not even walks for me at that time because I was still in a push-chair. But the size of the fields, the far distant horizons, the bunches of wild flowers we gathered and the inexhaustible song of the larks stayed with me more vividly than nursery rhymes. Hedgerows were heaped with the cream of may blossom; rivers were silver with fish or oozy with eels; rabbits, kingfishers, pheasants and lapwing were all part of my daily recovery. Even the nearby brickyard chimneys were living things, squeezing their smoke slowly on to the sky's palette, giving shades to an autumn sundown not seen anywhere else. And then school, and the years of being locked away in Victorian classrooms with high windows out of which I could only see the sky. The sky began to mean freedom. I daydreamt those years away longing for space and fields and the colour of hedgerows. At the age of five I might have been a poet if I'd had words to describe what my body felt. At ten I might have written about the silent avalanche of clouds at the end of our street, or the fields of jet-black corduroy. But I was afraid to put my thoughts into such words. We were not expected to use language like that. A spade was a spade and a cloud was a cloud, and corduroy trousers were worn by farm-labourers not fields. And then, at twenty, my first visit to Helpston and the discovery of Clare's poetry—thousands of poems all about the places and people and things I knew. People? Yes, I knew the woman in his sonnet 'Scandal', and 'The Mole-catcher', 'The Thresher', 'The Braggart', and 'The Foddering Boy'. They were of another generation but were, like the daisies and birds, direct descendants of the ones Clare had known. The realism with which he wrote about these subjects excited me:

She hastens out and scarcely pins her clothes
To hear the news and tell the news she knows
She talks of sluts marks each unmended gown
Herself the dirtiest slut in all the town . . .

*   *   *

Tattered and ragg'd with greatcoat tied in strings
And collared up to keep his chin from cold
The old mole-catcher on his journey sings
Followed by shaggy dog infirm and old . . .

*   *   *

With hand in waistcoat thrust the thresher goes
Early at morn to follow his employ
He nothing wants to know and nothing knows
And wearies life along with little joy . . .

Nor was Clare afraid to write about a rainy day either, when the land looks anything but golden:

So moping flat and low our valleys lie
So dull and muggy is our winter sky
Drizzling from day to day with threats of rain
And when that falls still threatening on again
From one wet week so great an ocean flows
That every village to an island grows . . .

He knew each mood of the year. The seasons have not changed. Crows still 'tumble up and down/At the first sight of Spring/And in old trees around the town/Brush winter from its wing.' And still in summer 'the ballad-singing larks now troop/By dozens from the hay/And dozens down as soon as up/Leaves one the time to play.' The sun (which Clare mentions over five hundred times) is still a very significant part of our land and remains, as it did for him, 'the unfettered sun' or 'hot, relentless sun', everything from 'the spoiling sun' to the 'pale splendour of a winter sun' constantly controlling our days. The sun was for Clare the beginning of life, the magician of seed and flower, the 'eternal ray' of hope. The harvest scenes may have changed but the tradition of harvest remains. And when summer is over the autumn returns with its own healing: 'There's nothing calms the unquiet mind/Like to the soothing of an autumn wind.' It is a season when the eye 'revels in wild delights', when 'every leaf of bush and weed/Is tipt with autumn's pencil now', where 'every object wears a changing hue' and 'naked fields hang lonely on the view'.

But it is, perhaps, in writing of winter that Clare excels. When he says ''Tis winter and I love to read indoors', I share the joy of settling down before a fire with a favourite book while outside 'The small wind whispers through the leafless hedge/Most sharp and chill.' From his cottage he would have looked out on a world that has a habit of withdrawing itself in December and January. The sky becomes hard and sullen as a frozen pond. The pheasant's cry bounces over it like a pebble on ice. The call of the wildfowl from a distant mere comes also from a secret past. Reeds shuffle along the dykes, their frosted banners all that remain of forgotten warriors. Flood water stutters its cold syllables against the hedge-roots. The vast sky goes into mourning and the snow begins to fall on 100,000 acres of sleeping farmland, slowly changing our world from black to white. And the excitement starts all over again.

I wrote in my first book *Portrait of the Fen Country*—'No part of the country can be isolated into a weekend or judged by a season, least of all the Fen country. After weeks of rain during sugar-beet lifting even the most ardent fen-lover will find his world damp and miserable. In winter the winds from the north-east can be so fierce and pitiless that you feel as if needles of ice are being thrown at your eyes. But in May when white mist hovers over young spring wheat the fens will feel as calm as a cathedral, and in summertime when the air is rich with the smells of meadowsweet and the first gold-rush of harvest it can be as perfect as Eden ever was.'

Clare taught me how to enjoy the seasons and the everyday things of life. Now, several books later, I can still say with him 'There is a breath—indeed there is/Of Eden left—I feel it now.'

When the late sun mellows the grey stone I see from my window, I remember the low sun lighting the bark on trees in woods he would have walked. When I see the bright clouds beyond the spires I feel as I did in my classroom and I long to escape. And now, unlike then, I can. Nothing can keep me from where I want to be and where I know I belong. Well, it would take more than a cold day or a persuasive invitation to try anywhere else.

Rhododendron Country: Sussex

FRANK TUOHY

Between the wars I grew up in Sussex, in a tamed, sometimes nearly suburban landscape. But the surroundings of childhood become imprinted; they bite into the memory. Certain images still return in dreams, and proclaim themselves the Ideal Country or the Great Good Place. A vision, perhaps, of stone-built houses near running water; among alder bushes, a water-splash deep enough for a small car—say, a bull-nosed Morris Cowley with wire-spoked wheels —to stall and refuse to budge. You scramble down barefoot, hesitate before putting your toes in the icy stream, and watch the minnows spark away in the clear-brown shallow waters. In the real world, though, such visions did not last. Suddenly there was a time when Wordsworth's intimations became Marxian symptoms: when earth and every common sight seemed ready with lessons in social development or economic history.

I grew up at a time, I suppose, when country life still centred round the 'carriage trade'. Even in a small town, the poor did their shopping in back streets. Their clothes, like their shoes, looked ill-fitting and uncomfortable. Poor people's skin was different, too—darker, weather-beaten. On Sundays, they went to churches and chapels built of corrugated iron. When they were ill, they crowded the surgery as 'panel patients'. In our district when you died, there were three women who might come to lay you out. One of them, however, only obliged at the best houses; another looked after the cottages. The third woman offered services and sympathy ('I wish you had got in to see her, she looked really lovely') to all of us in between: there were plenty in that category by that time.

I grew up only fifty miles from London. The county had quite recently been celebrated by Hilaire Belloc and Rudyard Kipling, as well as by numerous authors of guides to the Highways and By-ways of Weald and Downland. They described a world inhabited by iron smelters, trug-makers, sturdy yeomen and hunting squires. Our local craftsmen were genteel persons who had become herbalists, potters, weavers. Many of the big houses sheltered magnates from the Greek Islands or the Rand gold-fields. A maharaja, I think I remember, was Master of Hounds.

I grew up in a society whose traditions, true or false, had already gone. Instead of Belloc's yeomen quaffing the good ale, there were ex-officers who had commuted their pensions to start up chicken-farms; others, later, invested in whole ranges of sheds and wire-netting for mink or silver fox. A child thinks of his surroundings, however various, as permanent and of the people he knows as typical, however peculiar they may be. Every day some women delivered milk and cream from a 'model dairy farm'. At home in the middle of the morning, you would hear loud laughter from the drawing-room, and find Phyl and Ben, Eton-cropped, breeched and gaitered, looking like air aces left over from the war in Flanders. A jovial Siegfried, Phyl stood wide-legged before the fireplace; Ben, a moody oriental princeling, sat on the edge of a chair, letting cigarette ash fall inside the quite unobstructed curve offered by whipcord-covered thighs. These creatures were perplexing, it is true, but they were as much a part of country life as the Vicar, the Doctor with his five shouting daughters, the spiritualist Admiral or the Bible-punching Brigadier.

Now when I return there, I am conscious less of the inhabitants than of the special way in which the landscape itself has developed. Southwards from the Surrey hills you see the dark plantations everywhere: conifers, with *Cupressus* (*macrocarpa* and *leylandii*) predominant, monkey-puzzles, Portugal laurel. Most of all, rhododendron. Earlier generations had set their mansions on hill-tops or at the ends of avenues of lime or elm; cottages were huddled together in village streets. The rhododendron came with the rise of plutocracy. Profligate for a few weeks in the year, it produces those massed flower-clusters, frequently white and crimson, like ice-cream sundaes for which one's taste has palled. For the rest of the year, the rhododendron acts as a screen. In Sussex forty years ago, it screened off the ingrowing lives that sheltered beyond shut gates up a twisting drive, in houses where sometimes only the general prac-titioner, with his tablets and syringes, still called at the front door.

Now when I return, I notice that the rhododendrons have often grown straggly and have reverted to the original pinkish-mauve prototype. They no longer screen so successfully those big Edwardian villas, gabled and hung with terracotta tiles. One of these—it belonged to the Bible-punching Brigadier—has recently disappeared: a hoarding announces 'Luxury Development of 12 Regency Town Houses'. Others have become boarding-schools or summer headquarters for American colleges or religious organizations. Recently a number have brightened up noticeably: there's a Rover in the garage, and a fenced paddock where a pony is diligently exercising a plump schoolgirl. Not much has changed in all those years since we went to tea there with other children—snub surly boys, tanned wiry girls expert at tree-climbing—spending the holidays with grandmother while their parents were in India.

Now when I return, this region of shrubberies seems extraordinary in comparison with the open gardens of the American suburbs and university towns through which children and dogs run riot; or the *potagers* of the French countryside, or the courtyards of the south, where every plant has use or beauty. Only the Japanese resemble us in their affection for dull dark leaves—in their case, pines and azaleas—that look the same all the year round. To me the Sussex shrubberies show the gloomier side of middle-class life, its failure of warmth, its complete lack of fraternity; while the alder-hidden streams and the water-splash—which is still there, unchanged—represent the vision of happiness.

Three Sussex Poems

John Terraine

Countrymen

This is a sad poem, because the Royal Sussex Regiment (35th Foot) now no longer exists. The badge of the regiment was the tall, white plume of Roussillon. The 35th overthrew the Régiment de Roussillon on the Plains of Abraham outside Quebec on 12 September 1759. The English soldiers picked up the plumes from the hats of their fallen enemies and wore them as trophies.

Look at that tawny
Skin, hook nose,
Black villain's darting
Eye! What gypsy,
Moor or Spanish rover
Planted that face here?

This shockhead laugher,
Beaked like Caesar,
Is a bit more likely.
Here's a Saxon, sure enough—
Of sorts.

And this thick lump,
This bull, this
Bison—some sea-wolf sired
His lusty ancestors, no doubt.

And this one—ruddy-cheeked,
Green-fingered, sandy
Sly peasant mocking with his
Old grey cunning eyes.

You could raise a regiment of these fellows.
They'd poach a plume from Roussillon—or Hades;
They'd make a wrangle of it on any
Obstinate, bloody field.
You could call them:
'Royal Sussex'.

Amberley Wild Brooks in Flood

Grey like thin milk,
Taut under tense grey sky,
Rippled only by coot's wake
Or skim of gull—
The flood waters wait the coming of new rain.

207

Personal Map Reference

Drowned fence, drowned track,
Drowned tussock, drowned
The whole botanical collection
Of gaudy spring.

The water is waiting for rain
To whip its tight white surface into ecstasies,
For shrill excitement of wind
To sharpen its hunger;
And then the grey waste will march
Over sluice and dyke
To feed on flesh angrily:

The silent enemy.

Ghosts on the Downs

Across the deep breasts of the dappled Downs—

In the bright sunlight,
In cloud-shadow, speeding
Before unfriendly winds;
In the night-time
When owls do duty for the sleeping hawk;
Above all in twilight
Instants, heart-heaving
Dissolution
Of familiar shapes and understanding—

With the long leisure of eternity
Stroll the ancestral ghosts.

Their cold eyes dwell upon us.
Neutral the Bronze Age spearman;
Neutral the clanking Roman and the thegn;
Neutral the wide past of the windy uplands.

Always the wind; in its chill eye
The mute and unmoved survey of the ghosts.

Windover Hill

DIRK BOGARDE

It was about a mile from the cottage to his head, and all uphill. A little more than half-way, just as we had started to become a bit out of breath, there was the windmill. Nothing much was left of it, just a soft depression in the springy downland turf and a chalk and flint path fading into the grasses as it wandered down back to the lane. But the windmill was half-time for us, and we had a little sit-down to try and catch our breaths and to rest from the labour of having to carry the big black tin tray which banged our knees, or rather the knees of the one who was carrying it. We used to pick straws for who would take it on the first leg of the journey to the Giant, and swapped over at the windmill. So it was a rather important stop: and sometimes, if we had the grub-bag with us, we'd have a swig of Tizer or eat an apple before going on up. We called him the Giant. Most people just called him the Long Man, and that's how he was called on the postcards in the village. When we got to the top of Windover Hill we were very nearly at his head. Just Long Barrow and a few clumps of gorse and we were on the crest looking down his white outlined body standing legs astride, holding two poles or something.

We were on the top of Our World. Below us lay the beginning of the Weald through which the Cuckmere wound its way in wide loops like a silver chain glinting in the sun, nudging places to which we had rarely been like Upper Dicker, Michelham Priory, or Arlington where there was a house with a moat. But that lay well beyond Our World. Our boundary, fixed by the weakness or strength of our legs, was bounded, for all time, by Alfriston to the west, Wilmington to the north, Jevington to the east, and Litlington to the south. Within that frame all belonged to us. Or so we steadfastly believed for we shared it with few others. A shepherd from time to time chivvying his sheep gently across the thyme-scented turf towards Winchester's Pond, a very deep dew-pond from which, if once you slipped in, it was quite impossible to be extracted, so deep was it and so steep the sloping sides. The shepherd, Mr Dick, had told us this one April day when he showed us a cluster of pasque-flowers near

Snap Hill barn and how to dock the lambs' tails, which he did very easily be simply biting them off and tying them in neat bundles to dry out on the split-rail fences of the pens, to render them down later for tallow. Since he appeared to be a man of extreme knowledge we took his word for it and walked past the pond with the care and respect it obviously deserved.

Sometimes they'd be ploughing down on the flatter land near Lullington Court, and we'd see the gulls rise up behind the plough like scurries of torn paper, and in the late summer the wagons would come trundling up from the farm, pale pink and deep blue, the great horses shining sleek, their ears capped by little knitted woolly cones to keep away the flies.

These then were the only people with whom my sister and I shared Our World. Just Mr Dick, and the Aleford brothers stooking the corn, or stacking it into fat rectangular blocks as big as a cottage, to await the thatchers. No one else came there. Oh, to be sure, sometimes there would be a couple of what we used to call in those days, and this is almost fifty years ago, Hikers. We detested them. Scrawny people in coloured shirts and flapping shorts, with bags on their backs and maps in their hands. If we should chance upon one or two, and were far enough away to do so, we would hide. If come upon unawares, as sometimes we were, we just crossed our eyes violently, stuck out our tongues in a very reprehensible manner and ran screaming in the opposite direction. We'd never answer questions, and never even admit to being remotely sane. I think we secretly hoped that a couple of village idiots would frighten them off our territory back to the wickedness and debauchery of Eastbourne, miles away from Our World.

The reason that we made this long trek to the head of the Giant was quite simple. We slid down beside the length of him on the tin tray. It was a dizzying experience, and seldom ever fully accomplished. I had fixed a piece of rope through two holes at the side, and hanging on to this, with one or other of us giving a hefty shove to start the trip, we careered breathlessly from his head to far beyond his feet, ending up in a cornfield about thirty yards below. And that was that. Nothing much to it really, I suppose, but it was a never-failing delight, fraught with frightful dangers like falling off, which we did constantly, breaking your neck, cutting your knees on a

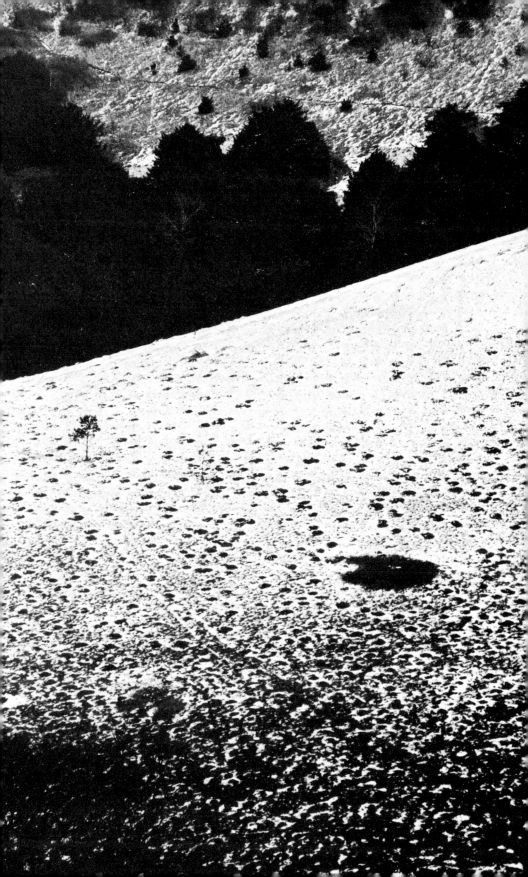

shard of flint, or hurtling into a dense thicket of hawthorn at his side, which was most disagreeable.

The first to go down (we drew straws, or grasses rather, for that too), had to drag the tray back up to the top again for the other rider. Which was not much fun and made you excessively hot, so the grub-bag was very useful, what with Tizer and apples. In a way, after the excitement of the ride, this was really perhaps the best part. You could just lie there in the grasses and listen to the wind wuthering gently above your head, the larks singing high in the blue intensity of the sky, the bleat of lambs and the clonkle-clankle of the sheep bells. There was no other sound.

From here, leaning upon your elbows, you could look down across the distant water-meadows draining into the Cuckmere through little streams and dykes which looked like silver cracks in green paint, and to your left was the small huddle of red roofs which was Milton Street where there was a pub with its name considerately printed in big white letters across the tiles. The Royal Oak. There wasn't a church there, but a mile beyond, across the fields, the spire of Berwick church poked above embowering elms, and far beyond that, blue in the haze of summer, the bulk of Firle Beacon thrust into the Weald like the prow of an upturned boat. Half a mile north of Wilmington the railway from Lewes to Eastbourne ran across the flat land; but you really hardly saw it, except when an occasional engine trundled past pulling two coaches, and puffing little snorts of white smoke which drifted across the meadows like wisps of goose-down, and which faded into the stillness of the morning.

Even in the winter the view from Our World was very beautiful, when the downs were softly silvered with the first frosts, and the ice lay along the edge of the river glittering in the pale orange sun like crushed glass. The trees were black and twisted by the winds which raced in from the sea, sending the low clouds scudding fast towards the far horizon where, in the clear winter light, the harsh, heathy ridge of Ashdown Forest lay like a black chalk-line across the umber and blue of the woods below. We hardly ever saw the forest in the summer because the haze blurred it into the fields and sky. But in the winter it seemed that you could see for miles and miles, and the whole Weald would lie under plough below our feet, spread out like a great patchwork quilt of moleskin and corduroy; cocoa-coloured, brown, sienna, and where the chalk was heaviest, milk-chocolate. Here and there a tidy rectangle of winter wheat showing hesitant green, and dotted all about were the amber stacks of corn or barley.

But the summer was best. The summer always was. With corn-cockles in the fields, poppies in great scarlet drifts, and little clouds of Chalk Blues going up before us as we walked over the soft sheep-cropped turf on our way home. We would cut down the hill, through the lower fields, on to the chalk road to Wilmington Priory and then double back to Milton Street and the Royal Oak. There, in the backyard amidst crates of empty bottles and beer barrels smel-ling sourly in the sun, stood six wooden beehives with thatched roofs, and for sixpence we would buy a fresh honeycomb which the innkeeper, swathed in net, took from the hive as we watched from a respectful distance. And then, for two pence, we would buy a warm brown loaf from his wife who had baked it not long before in the bake-house beside the privy. With our purchases safely in the grub-bag we would walk along the road, the tray over my shoulder, and climb the grassy track home to the cottage. The three square miles of our domain contained many other enchantments apart from warm brown loaves and honeycombs: there was also sweet, cold tea in fat green bottles, and cold meat patties with cheese and pickled onions which the Aleford brothers shared with us at harvest-time when we joined their wives and daughters in the gleaning.

Armed with wooden rakes, bare legs in wellingtons against the razor cuts of the stubble, we gathered up the fallen barley stalks into neat bundles and bound them tight with rough twine; a scattering of us walking across the broad field behind the rattle and clatter of the machine, the women in old straw hats, the children gathering great bunches of deep blue cornflowers, the elms standing tall and cool along the hedgerow where the tea and the patties were stored in wicker baskets thatched with fresh green grasses. Sometimes Mr Ben would let out a holler above the rattle and clang and we'd find the neat ball of a field-mouse's nest spilled among the tumbled stalks. Once I put a whole family into the pocket of my shorts, but they nibbled through and fell into my wellingtons and there was a terrific fuss of laughter and cheers and pulling and pushing; and often a hare zigzagged away across the stubble, leaping and looping with the dogs in full cry until they lost him on the soft flank of the downs above the barley field.

As the sun sank beyond the Beacon, we gathered up the gleanings, the wicker baskets, the rakes and balls of twine, and everyone clambered into the long wagon for the journey home to Litlington and The Court. At the road we jumped off, for we lived in the other direction, and with our bundles slung over our shoulders we waved them down the chalky hill until they were out of sight, their voices light and high above the creak and the crunch of the wagon's wheels in the soft evening air, three of the girls from Litlington singing 'Ramona' in harmony. Then up our track among high hedges with the early bats out, swooping and wheeling across the apricot sky, and the first whisper of an evening breeze whiffling through the campion and fool's parsley. A day well spent and, as young Mrs Ben had said, enough barley gleaned to feed ten hens and a cockerel or brew a pint of ale. A slow, sweet, gentle England.

*   *   *

I first saw Our World in 1927 when I was six and my father had walked me up to the windmill to show me what he called the 'most beautiful place in all England', and I knew then that it was. It was 'ours' for over a decade, and every hedge, thicket, track or tumulus which it contained became our personal, and very private, property. Sadly, in 1938, we left, and for one reason and another I never went back again until one autumn day in 1960.

I stood on the top of the Giant and looked about me. Topographically, little seemed to have changed, but childhood, along with much else, had gone forever. White bricks outlined the Giant now: wire fences surrounded him, the soft downland grass was thick and coarse, stuck about with thistle and ragwort, gorse had cruelly scabbed the smooth sides of Windover Hill, for no sheep ever grazed here now, and there was no Mr Dick with smock, crook, and gaitered trousers to chivvy them towards the green sludge which once had been Winchester's Pond. Electric pylons marched across the Weald past Arlington and Chalvington, and Polegate, once just a crossroads and a bus stop, was beribboned with cheap bungalows spreading south to make Willingdon a reluctant suburb of Eastbourne. The High Street of Alfriston, which had rung to the cheerful cries of Potato Pete and Fred the Fish, on Tuesdays and Fridays respectively, as they pushed their barrows up to the Market Cross, now rumbled with tourists who, spewed from dirty coaches, jammed the warming-panned tea-shoppes or bought cheap pottery, postcards and oven-gloves in the carefully 'restored' quaintness of ugly little boutiques.

It is always unwise to go back. I regretted my return bitterly. Better by far just to remember it as it once had been and would never be again. But one is a prisoner of one's past, and particularly of one's early childhood, and the temptation to 'have another look' had proved too strong for me. Alas! However, from the top of Our World, which once had been 'the most beautiful place in all England' it looked almost, almost the same. The wind whipped in from the sea, speeding low clouds raggedly across the whale-backed downs on which I stood, just as it always had done, the upturned prow of Firle Beacon still poked gently into the Weald, rooks swung high, planeing out over the copse at Hunters Burgh, and far below the serpentine Cuckmere gleamed like pewter in the fast-fading light. It was nearly all the same. But it, and I, had grown older.

Black Mountains

RAYMOND WILLIAMS

1

See this layered sandstone among the short mountain grass. Place your right hand on it, palm downward. See where the sun rises and where it stands at noon. Direct your middle finger midway between them. Spread your fingers, not widely. You now hold this place in your hand.

The six rivers rise in the plateau of the back of your hand. The first river, now called Mynwy or Monnow, flows at the outside edge of your thumb. The second river, now called Olchon, flows between your thumb and the first finger, to join the Mynwy at the top of your thumb. The third river, now called Honddu, flows between your first and second fingers and then curves to join the Mynwy, away from your hand. The fourth river, now called Grwyne Fawr, flows between your second and third fingers, and then curves the other

215

way, joining the fifth river, now called Grwyne Fechan, that has been flowing between your third and your little finger. The sixth river, now called Rhiangoll, flows at the outside edge of your little finger. Beyond your hand are the two rivers to the sea. Mynwy carrying Olchon and Honddu flows into the circling Wye. Grwyne and Rhiangoll flow into the Usk. Wye and Usk, divided by the Forest of Gwent, flow to the Severn Sea.

It was by Wye and Usk, from the Severn Sea and beyond it, that men first came to this place.

The ridges of your five fingers, and the plateau of the back of your hand, are now called the Black Mountains. Your thumb is Crib y Gath or Cat's Back. Your first finger is Haterall. Your second finger is Ffawyddog, with Bal Mawr at the knuckle. Your third finger is Gader, with Gader Fawr at the knuckle. Your little finger is Allt Mawr, and its nail is Crug Hywel, giving its name to Crickhowell below it. On the back of your hand are Twyn y Llech and Twmpa and Rhos Dirion and Waun Fach. Mynwy and Olchon flow from Twyn y Llech. Honddu flows from Twyn y Llech and Twmpa. Grwyne Fawr flows from Rhos Dirion. Grwyne Fechan and Rhiangoll flow from Waun Fach.

You hold the shapes and the names in your hand.

2

It was by Wye and Usk, from the Severn Sea and beyond it, that men first came to this place.

We have no ready way to explain ourselves to you. Our language has gone utterly, except for the placename which you now say as Ewyas. The names by which we knew ourselves are entirely unknown to you. We left many marks on the land but the only marks that you can easily recognize are the long stone graves of our dead. If you wish to know us you must learn to read the whole land.

3

The long barrows of the first Black Mountain shepherds are clustered on flat grasslands between the steep northern scarp, at your wrist, and on one side the wide valley of the Wye, on the other the valley of the Usk and the basin of Llyn Syvadon, now called Llan-gorse Lake.

When the first shepherds came there was thick oak forest from the rivers to the level of these grasslands. Then the forest thinned, and there was good pasture among the scattered trees. On the ridges above them, in the climate of that time, there were great winter bogs in the peat above the deep sandstone, but there was some summer grazing on the slopes. They lived at that chosen level, at first only in the summers, going back to the rivers in the winters, but later yearthrough.

These are still flat grasslands, grazed by thousands of sheep and hundreds of ponies. Below them and above them the land has changed and been changed.

4

We can count in generations. Say two hundred and twenty generations from the first shepherds to us. Then a new people came. Say one hundred and sixty generations from them to us. They came when the climate was changing. Winters were much colder and summers hotter and drier. While elsewhere in the island men were moving down from chalk uplands, because the springs were failing, here the sandstone ridges and the plateau were drying, and there was new summer grazing. Surviving tracks show the change. To every ridge, now, there are long transverse, sometimes zigzag, tracks from the middle heights to the crests. They are often sunken, making a characteristic notch where they break the ridge. The local name for such a track is *rhiw*. Along these tracks, sheep and cattle were driven for the summer grazing. Meanwhile, below the old grasslands, the forest was changing. The damp oak forest fell back, and new clearings were made among the more diverse woods. And this people felled along the slopes of the ridges. There was then more grass but also the heather began to spread. They lived and worked in these ways for sixty generations.

5

New peoples came. Say a hundred generations from them to us. And again the climate was changing. Winters were milder, summers cooler and wetter. They settled a little higher than the first shepherds, and in new ways. They built folds and camps at the ends of ridges: at Pentwyn, Y Gaer, Crug Hywel, Castell Dinas. There were summer pastures behind them, along the lower ridges, for their sheep and cattle and horses. And still they cleared towards the valleys, in small square fields. There were peaceful generations, but increasingly, now, more peoples were coming from the east. The folds and steadings became armed camps. The names of history begin with the Silures. But then a different arrival: an imperial people: Romans. These said of the Silures: 'non atrocitate, non clementia mutabatur': changed neither by cruelty nor by mercy. Literate history, imperial history, after more than a hundred generations of history.

6

In literate history the Black Mountains are marginal. They are still classified today as marginal or as waste land. After the Silures no new people settled them. The tides of conquest or lordship lapped to their edges and their foothills, leaving castles facing them—Ewyas Harold, Ewyas Lacy, Grosmont, Skenfrith, White Castle, Abergavenny, Crickhowell, Bronllys, Hay, Clifford—to command their peoples. Romans drove military roads at their edges. Normans pushed closer, but had no use for land above seven hundred feet. In the mountains and their valleys the people were still there, with their animals. They were the children of the first shepherds and of the upland people and of the camp-builders. Roman governors wanted them to come down and live in new towns. Some went, some stayed. When the Romans left the island, some came back to the mountains. By at latest the sixth century, in modern reckoning, the Black Mountains were a kingdom, which lasted, precariously, until the twelfth century. Twenty generations of Roman rule and its aftermath. Twenty-five generations of a small native kingdom. They called the kingdom by a very old name: Ewyas.

Where then are the Black Mountains? The physical answer is direct. The literate and administrative answer is more difficult.

At a certain point on the narrow and winding road which we drive in summer for shopping—past Pentwyn and Parc y Meirch, below the source of the Mynwy and over the brooks of Dulas and Esgyrn—at a certain point on this secluded road between high banks and hedges of hazel and holly and thorn, at this indistinguishable point there is a ridged bump in the roadway, where the roadmen of Brecon (now Powys) and the roadmen of Hereford (now Hereford and Worcester) have failed to see eye to eye. It is a trivial unevenness, deep within this specific region. It is the modern border between England and Wales.

And this is how it has gone, in literate and administrative history. The small kingdom of Ewyas—not small if you try to walk it, but politically small—was often, while it still had identity, redrawn or annexed or married into the neighbouring kingdoms of Brycheiniog or Gwent or Erging (Archenfield). Its modern political history is differently arbitrary. A dispute between the London court and a local landowning family, at the time of the Act of Union between England and Wales, led to a border which follows no natural feature or, rather, several in an incomprehensible series. In the twentieth century, three counties had lines drawn across and through the Black Mountains: lines on maps and in a few overgrown and lichened stones. Brecon pushed one way, Monmouthshire another, Hereford a third. The first was part of Wales, the third part of England; Monmouthshire, until it became Gwent, anomalous between them. A national park boundary followed these amazing administrative lines. Then Brecon was incorporated into the new Powys. Monmouthshire in name became the old Gwent. Hereford and Worcester, unwillingly joined, considered and rejected the name of West Mercia. It was almost, even in name, a very old situation: this marginal, this waste land, taken in at the very edges of other, more powerful, units.

Within the Black Mountains, these lines on the map mean nothing. You have only to stand there to see an unusually distinct and specific region. Or go on that midsummer Sunday—Shepherds' Sunday—when they drive the tups from above the Usk to above the

Monnow and track down unmarked sheep. An old internal organization, in the region's old activity, still visibly holds. Later, of course, the externally drawn lines and their consequences arrive, administratively, in the post. They are usually bills.

8

How to see it, physically? At first it is so strange. You need your hand on the stone to discern its extraordinary structure. Within the steep valleys, or from any of the ridges, this basic shape of the hand is not visible. And of course at every point there are minor features: cross valleys, glaciated cwms, rockfalls (*darens*), steeply gouged watercourses. It is so specific a country, yet its details take years to learn.

Black mountains? From a distance, like others, they are blue. From very close they are many colours: olive-green under sunlight; darker green with the patches of summer bracken; green with a reddish tinge when there are young leaves on the whinberries; dark with the heather out of flower, purple briefly in late summer; russet in the late autumn bracken; a pale gold, often, in the dead winter bracken, against the white of snow. Black? Entirely so, under heavy storm clouds. Very dark and suddenly solid under any thick cloud. The long whaleback ridges can be suddenly awesome.

But then their valleys are so different. Now Mynwy and Olchon and Honddu and Rhiangoll are farmed; Grwyne Fawr is forested and dammed; Grwyne Fechan is farm, a little forest and then upland pasture. The oldest modern farms are half-way up each slope from the valley beds, where the springs mostly rise. The old valley roads are at this level. But there are now roads and farms right down by the rivers, where there can be some flat fields. Then from these and the others the cleared fields climb the slopes, to uneven heights. Ash and thorn and rowan and cherry are still felled, bracken ploughed, to enclose a new field from the mountain. Others, once cleared, have gone back to scrub and bracken. At the farthest points, often surprisingly close, are old ruined stone farms, thick now with the nettles marking human occupation. In the Napoleonic wars there was this high and intensive settlement. It fell back with the decline of the Welsh woollen industry. The fields have been taken in to other farms. The rest of the story is what is called depopulation.

But the valleys are bright green, under the different colours of the mountains. Trees flourish in them. From some ridges the valleys still look like woodland, with the farms in clearings. But there is always a sharp contrast between the bleak open tops, with their heather and whinberry and cotton sedge and peat pools, their tracks which dissolve into innumerable sheep tracks, their sudden danger, in bad weather, in low cloud and mist with few landmarks, and the green settled valleys, with the fine trimmed farm hedges, the layered sandstone houses—colours from grey and brown towards pink or green, the patchwork of fields. At midsummer the valleys are remarkable, for on the trimmed hedges of thorn and holly and hazel and ash and field maple there is an amazing efflorescence of stands of honeysuckle and pink or white wild roses, and on the banks under them innumerable foxgloves. It is so close to look up from these flowers to the steep ridges. By one of the ruined farms there was once a whole field of foxgloves. It is now back to bracken and thistle. But in the next field they are felling and clearing again, and the ploughed earth above the sandstone goes through a range of colours from wet dark red to dried pink among the bright grass.

So this extraordinarily settled and that extraordinarily open wild country are very close to each other and intricately involved. Either, with some strictness, can be called pastoral, but then with very different implications. As the eye follows them, in this unusually defining land, the generations are distinct but all suddenly present.

9

It is a place where you can stand and look out. From Haterall there is the vast patchwork of fields of the Herefordshire plain, across to the Malverns and the Clees. From Twmpa there is distance after distance of upland Wales, from Radnor and Eppynt to Plynlimmon and Cader Idris and the neighbouring Beacons. From Allt Mawr there is the limestone scarp, on the other side of the Usk, where the iron industry came, and in the valleys behind it, Rhymney and Taff and Rhondda, the mining for coal.

Land, labour, and history. It can be cold standing there. The winds sweep those ridges. You go back down, into the settled valleys, with their medley of map names.

Different views, different lives. But occasionally, laying your right hand, palm downward, on the deep layered sandstone, you know a whole, intricate, distinct place. The Black Mountains. Ewyas.

Walking Over Grabbist

R. N. CURREY

When we, by the almost obsolete
Placing of foot before foot have raised
Our eyes to gorse and bracken, then we may
Look round a moment on a world that was.

This track once shouldered wagons from Minehead.
Two preachers with one horse would come this way,
One riding and one walking; country people
Carried their sweat to church and chapel then.

Below, in the easy prose of wheels,
We ride the metalled roads, but now, up here,
Breathing the heather and the distance, feel
The measured, springing feet of poetry stir.

Two Rivers

ANTHONY THWAITE

Blue frozen ox-heart, bleeding down a cleft
Between rock towers and turrets, execution-place
Whose issue is a frontier; first a trickle
Threaded through pulpy ice, then spinning pebbles
Churned into soapy foam, then settling down
To placid valley, bridged and tractable,
Where it becomes a continent in tribute.

Far to the west is home: three miles upstream
This one begins in reeds, is lost in meadows,
Gathers itself discreetly, winds through shallows,
Nowhere remarked except where minor roads
Pretend a ford, or boys paddle and shout.
Known to five parishes, two dozen farms,
It flows towards a sea it does not know.

From Cotswold to Chiltern

RICHARD FITTER

When I first came to live in the Chilterns, after seven years in the
Cotswolds, I was greatly struck by the contrast between these two
ranges of calcareous hills that watch each other across the Vales of
Oxford and Aylesbury. Instead of wide-skied ploughlands criss-
crossed by stone walls, I found ramparts of beechwoods, and smal-
ler, hedge-bound fields. Instead of villages all built of honey-brown
or rufous limestone, I found the characteristic flint-lined walls and
cottages of the chalk. Instead of being almost confined to lanes and
roads, I found a network of footpaths through the woods and up
and down the escarpment.

223

Some of the contrasts, of course, were due to my moving from the dip-slope of the Cotswolds, at Burford, to the escarpment of the Chilterns, at Chinnor. Burford nestles in the Windrush valley at the eastern end of what often seemed to be a windswept plateau not so far from the North Pole. Chinnor lies at the foot of the scarp, but my new house was on the summit, with a view that encompassed not only the Berkshire Downs west to the White Horse, but also the Faringdon Folly, Boars Hill, and the long line of the Cotswolds. I could see Blackheath Clump a couple of miles north of Burford, and when the sky was really clear I could even just make out that mile-long row of beeches on the hillside west of Northleach. Such a change in perspective, from the confines of Sheep Street to the whole spread of the Vale of White Horse and the southern part of the Vale of Aylesbury was most invigorating.

As a Londoner I was intrigued to find myself living at the western edge of what seems to have been the Romano-British hunting territory of Londinium, whose jurisdiction, in this respect at least, apparently extended to the Chiltern escarpment. So here I was, as far into the country as a Londoner might legitimately go. Not that I wanted to hunt anything in the conventional sense, only in the sense that a naturalist is always hunting.

The Chilterns lie in four counties, Bedfordshire, Hertfordshire, Buckinghamshire, and Oxfordshire, with boundaries unaltered by the recent shake-up. Within a mile of my home the boundary between Bucks and Oxon runs slantingly down the scarp out past a Roman site and across the plain in such a way as to suggest it has been there ever since the last Roman left his farm. That may have been later than elsewhere, for a Romano-British enclave persisted in the Chilterns for a couple of centuries after the Saxons had settled the Thames gravels below. Since then, the Chilterns have rejoiced in having no history at all, in the conventional sense. Since the Conqueror swooped on Berkhamsted, no battles seem to have been fought for its towns or in its forests; nobody has even suggested that Mons Badonicus must be somewhere in the Chilterns, as they have in many places just across the Thames in Berkshire. Much of the Civil War took place in the plain at the Chiltern foot but although John Hampden was born at Hampden House up on the hill, he fought and died in the plain, at Chalgrove Field and Thame. No, the history of the Chilterns has been the history of the common people, which few ever bother to chronicle; the men who felled the plateau oakwoods to send down the Thames to fuel London's fires; the men who replanted the woods to beech, to provide the basis of the High Wycombe chair trade; the old bodgers who worked on chair legs and arms out in the woodlands away from High Wycombe; the generations of farmers who farmed the fields their ancestors carved out of the wildwood.

But the wildwood itself, the primeval forest of England, that must have clothed most of these hills when the first Saxons came down the Icknield Way, has gone. Although the Chilterns are still one of the most thickly wooded parts of England, not a square yard of woodland can really claim to be primeval. It has all been cut out more than once. Even such a wood as Bledlow Great Wood, mentioned in Domesday Book, has almost certainly been either replanted or at least allowed to regenerate, more than once. Then there is the mystery of the Chiltern beeches. Just how native are they, and did they exist away from the escarpment in former days? Nobody really knows, but it seems certain that there was once a great deal more oak in the Chilterns than there now is, and we know that a lot of beech was planted in the eighteenth and nineteenth centuries.

To a naturalist like myself the wildlife of the Chilterns has always seemed greatly superior to that of the Cotswolds. Bare open arable fields offer few attractions to the bird-watcher, for instance, apart from stone curlews, partridges, skylarks and corn buntings, and the Chilterns have those too. Woodland always has more to offer, and the small, rather scrubbed up patches of chalk grassland so common in the Chilterns have more still, yielding between them a good range of warblers, tits, nuthatches and other song birds. True, the Chilterns have nothing to compare with the valleys of the Windrush and Evenlode, for most of the Chiltern valleys are dry, at least in their upper reaches. I have never seen whinchats in the Chilterns, as I used to in the Windrush valley below Burford, or, except as a flash in the pan, redstarts, as I used to regularly in Wychwood Forest. Both Chiltern woodlands and Wychwood, however, provide that splendid spectacle of the roding woodcock, pursuing its wide arc across the tree-tops while uttering its two diverse call-notes, the shrill 'twissick, twissick' and the curious little growl.

When it comes to wild flowers, especially orchids, the Chilterns really assert their primacy. They have more species, especially of the rare ones, than any other district in Britain, except East Kent. The ghost orchid is now found in two or three places in the Chilterns alone, having vanished from its Welsh Border haunts many years since. The red helleborine, the (sadly diminishing) glory of the Cotswolds, also has its Chiltern locality, though it has not flowered there recently. The military orchid we share with Suffolk (three sites to one), and the monkey orchid with Kent. We even a few years ago had a single lady orchid, that special glory of Kent, but this too has disappeared. Most people never see the rare orchids, but they do see the common ones of the chalk turf: pale lilac spotted orchids, deeper pink-purple fragrant orchids, bright magenta-pink pyramidals, and the very curious bee orchid, whose lower lip so closely resembles the rear of a small bumble bee apparently sipping nectar from the flower. The common ones of the woodlands are less exciting, though the large white helleborine has a severe beauty of its own and the other helleborines repay a close examination to see the delicate colouring of their subfusc flowers.

The chalk turf of the Chilterns has its specialities too, white wild candytuft and purple Chiltern gentian, a larger version of the common autumn gentian, besides those commoner wild flowers that give such a blaze of colour to the late summer chalk grasslands: deep purple clustered bellflower, paler purple marjoram, blue scabious, yellow hawkbits and white wild carrot. In the woodlands, it is spring that brings the colour displays, sheets of white wood-anemones and sweet woodruff, yellow primroses, and hyacinth-coloured bluebells. The chalk turf too has its spring glories, especially the blue-violet of the hairy violet and the yellow of the cowslips.

All in all it is the great variety of the Chiltern landscapes that appeals to me most. In the north are the steep bare escarpments, as at Ivinghoe Beacon, and steep wooded escarpments, as at Bledlow and Chinnor. Further south, along the banks of the Thames, the escarpment flattens out, and between Ipsden and Goring, and between Marlow and Bourne End, great open fields sweep down to the river with an almost Cotswold air. There is contrast too between the hanging woodlands of the escarpment and the many inland dry valleys, such as the one which runs from Princes Risborough to West Wycombe, and the plateau woodlands, such as those around the Hampdens. On the steep slopes there is almost no soil, and the beeches are shallow-rooted; so too are the many ash saplings that spring up before the beech can get going. The ashes soon fail, because they need deep soil, but the beeches keep going and dominate them in the end. On the plateau, however, the soil is deep over the clay-with-flints, and here the ash never gets a chance; beech outstrips it. The beech is a really dominant tree, so that those other tree glories of the Chilterns, the wild cherry and the whitebeam, usually only manage to push their way in at the edge of a beech-wood or when grassland is growing up from scrub. If I had to choose one week out of the year to be about in the Chilterns, it would not be the one at the end of October when all the beeches turn fiery orange, but the one at the very end of April or the beginning of May, when the pale green young beech leaves are bursting all around, the wood edges turn white with cherry blossom, and the silvery young leaves of the whitebeams glisten against the apple-green of the thorn bushes on the steep escarpment slopes.

Points of View in Dorset

JOHN STEWART COLLIS

1

I got off my bicycle and stared at it. It would last five minutes at most, then it would be gone and not seen any more. It had never been before, it would never be again, its existence five minutes. Such is the difference between what we see in the heavens and what we see on earth. We call the hills everlasting. In our lifetime anyway they are always there. We grow up, we go away, we find all things inconstant, we become maddened by the filthy rags of change and decay that drape the skeletons of hope and joy. We return to the mountains. All is the same. They are constant. And so great is the virtue in that constancy that as we gaze upon them, many years and many stains are wiped away from our hearts.

But see those mountainous places in the sky, such shape, such style, such promise, that if only they belonged to land we could reach them and find happiness for evermore! Alas, they are no more substantial than visions of better days. They are held aloft for a bare five minutes. Maybe sometimes no one sees them. Perhaps I alone saw this one from a field in Dorset. A cloud, black as ink, shaped like a map of England, screened the sun, and its rims were bright with a whiteness more radiant than anything I have seen before. Thus was the mighty map margined with blazing silver shores. In a few moments the picture was taken down. It would never be exhibited again.

2

Again!
The chestnut tree lights up the candles
at whose signal oak and beech,
elm, plane, and lime,
and the witch-like fingers of the ash,
each in its own time
produce from barenness,
weave from that wood
silky flakes of green!

3

I am not cast out.
I am received by Nature.
Here the Age of Man upon the Earth
recedes into the silence.
Here is the power that can endure
our play, our pilgrimage,
our coming and departure.

But I am not cast out.
No doubly-chiselled cliffs nor monstrous snow
disallow my presence by their might
to minimize the human.
Here stamp not those peaks that glow
in the first and the last light
not shed for men below.

I am received by these slopes.
They are more powerful than any peak
To chasten and subdue Man's pride
in flaring shallow conquest.
They do more than humble. They speak
in answer to our prayer,
and show us what we seek.

4

Leave me alone Muse! Let me enjoy things for once without having
to put them down on paper. When, after this rainy day, I see a
sudden break in the sky behind the hill, like an announcement of the
reign of peace, its beams throwing to the sea a light not laid upon the
land, and kindling on the fields what shines not from the
waves—don't require me to say it, Muse, leave me alone. When I
pass over the hill and see a copse below looking like a pair of
trousers, let me fail to observe the similitude, and see the wood
because of the trees. When I look down across the bulging pastures,
many of them shaped exactly like enormous beautifully made beds
with green sheets, don't make me do anything about it, Muse, let me
simply enjoy what I see. When a dense flock of starlings gives the
impression of a flying carpet; when a squirrel runs up a tree with the
same celerity as it runs down it; when in the morning sunlight after a
severe frost every single blade of grass on the lawn, if closely looked
at, is seen as an erect white caterpillar—for heaven's sake don't
insist on my taking a note of this. Let me off. Leave me alone, Muse!

INDEX OF CONTRIBUTORS
AND BIOGRAPHICAL NOTES

Index of Contributors

BROWNJOHN, ALAN 62

Born in 1931 and a member of a distinguished generation of poets which includes Ted Hughes, Geoffrey Hill, and George MacBeth. Collections of his work first appeared in the Sixties—*The Railings, The Lions' Mouths*—and his latest poems, *A Night in the Gazebo*, were published in 1980.

COBB, RICHARD 12

Professor of Modern History at Oxford. A Francophile of the most extraordinary kind, his investigation of the revolutionary years has broken through the conventions to reveal an eighteenth-century world in which ordinary men and women walk and talk—and shift the levers of destiny. His *A Sense of Place* and *Tour de France*, and a new book, *Promenades*, are historical essays for the connoisseur.

COLLIS, JOHN STEWART 227

Born in 1900 and, as Michael Holroyd said, one of those rare writers who is able to dispense information in the language of the imagination. He is the scholar-poet who deals in facts and philosophy, and his *The Worm Forgives the Plough* is one of the great descriptions of English rural life.

CURREY, R. N. 222

One of a group of South African writers who came here during the Thirties—they included William Plomer and Laurens van der Post—and a celebrated poet of the Second World War. He has written *This Other Planet, Tiresias and Other Poems, Poems from India* (edited with R. V. Gibson) and *Poets of the 1939–1945 War*.

FITTER, RICHARD 223

Author and naturalist. Has helped to run many conservationist bodies and is at present secretary of the Fauna Preservation Society. His works include *London's Natural History, Finding Wild Flowers*, and *Vanishing Wild Animals of the World*.

GIROUARD, MARK 182

Born in 1931. Was Slade Professor of Fine Art at Oxford 1975–6, and has written *The Victorian Country House, Life in the English Country House*, and *Historic Houses of Britain*.

Index of Contributors

GITTINGS, ROBERT   69

Born in Portsmouth in 1911, the son of a naval surgeon. Poet and literary biographer, his lives of John Keats and Thomas Hardy reveal a brilliant understanding of the creative personality. His *Collected Poems* were published in 1978 and he has analysed his own art in *The Nature of Biography*.

HAWKES, JACQUETTA   163

Born and educated in Cambridge, where she read Archaeology and Anthropology. Now married to the novelist J. B. Priestley. Her archaeological works include *A Land* and *Prehistoric Britain*, and in 1979 she published an autobiographical novel, *A Quest of Love*.

HAYTER, ALETHEA   178

Born in Cairo in 1911. She has written *Mrs Browning: A Poet's Work and its Setting*, *A Sultry Month: Scenes of London Literary Life in 1846*, *Horatio's Version* and, most recently, has edited Edward Fitzgerald's letters.

HILL, SUSAN   80

Born in Yorkshire in 1942. Wrote a remarkable series of novels in her twenties whilst living in solitude in Aldeburgh, Suffolk during the winter months. Her stories include, *A Change for the Better*, *I'm the King of the Castle*, *Strange Meeting* and *The Bird of Night*.

HILLABY, JOHN   187

Walking has become the rarest form of travel, alas, but if anything can change this, John Hillaby's thoughtful, intellectual and pleasure-giving soliloquies as he walks the world should be able to. He has described this very personal travel in *Journey to the Jade Sea*, *Journey Through Britain*, and *Journey Through Love*.

HOBAN, RUSSELL   57

Born in Lansdale, Pennsylvania but came to live in London some twenty or so years ago, where he has established himself as a remarkably original novelist and also as a children's writer of genius—*The Mouse and His Child*. His novels include *The Lion of Boaz-Jachin and Jachin-Boaz*, *Turtle Diary*, and *Riddley Walker*.

Countryside, and that remarkable examination of conservationist policies and where they are taking us, *The Common Ground*. He has also edited Gilbert White's *Natural History of Selborne* and is currently working on a study of Richard Jefferies.

MacBeth, George   8

One of the finest voices of the P. J. Kavanagh, Derek Walcott, Ted Hughes generation, his collections of poetry include *The Broken Places* and *A Doomsday Book*. He lives in Norfolk.

May, Derwent   113

Literary Editor of *The Listener*, naturalist, and novelist. His novels include *The Professionals*, *Dear Parson*, and *The Laughter in Djakata*. One of his important places—the Blackwater estuary.

Middleton, Stanley   140

Began writing in the late 1950s. Since then has established himself as a novelist of extraordinary ability. His works include *Harris's Requiem*, *The Golden Evening*, *Cold Gradations*, and *Holiday*, which won the Booker Prize. These stories reflect with a quiet accuracy many of the developments in English society over the last thirty years, particularly in connection with people whose higher education has moved them out of family traditions and manners.

Mohanti, Prafulla   171

Lives partly in his native Orissa and partly in London. Trained at Leeds as an architect, he is also an artist, dancer, and writer whose work reflects two cultures. His rural origins are movingly described in *My Village, My Life* and delightfully in *Indian Village Tales*. He writes with the country story-teller's simplicity and purity.

Moorhouse, Geoffrey   91

Journalist and travel-writer in the classic tradition of going through it all yourself before setting it down. His books include *The Press*, *Against All Reason*, *The Missionaries*, *The Fearful Void*, and *The Boat and The Town*. The latter work shows his powers of description.

Morris, Jan   146

Lives in Wales and one of the most evocative exponents of places now writing. Books include *Venice*, *Oxford*, *The Presence of*

Spain, and the *Pax Britannica* trilogy (*Pax Britannica*, *Heaven's Command*, and *Farewell the Trumpets*). She has also edited *The Oxford Book of Oxford*, an anthology of the city.

NICHOLSON, NORMAN   144

Born in Millom, Cumberland, and continues to live there, and in the same house. In fact he acknowledges how this little town on the edge of Wordsworth territory has fed his poetic imagination since childhood. His debt to it reaches a noble climax in *A Local Habitation*. He has also written two witty autobiographical books about Millom, *Provincial Pleasures* and *Wednesday Early Closing*.

PITTER, RUTH   5

Born in 1897 and published her first book of poetry in 1920. Her places are a sacred territory, a land in which the seventeenth-century metaphysical poets would know their way around. Her *Collected Poems* were published in 1968 and she received the Queen's Gold Medal for Poetry in 1955.

PYM, BARBARA   119

Died in January 1980 and her contribution to this anthology was among the last of her literary acts. A novelist of unique gifts, the story of how she was dropped by her publishers and forgotten for over a decade, then restored to deserved fame by her percipient admirers, is now a legend. Her novels include *Excellent Women*, *A Glass of Blessings*, and *Quartet in Autumn*. Her final book was *A Few Green Leaves*, published after her death.

READ, PIERS PAUL   32

Born in 1941, the third son of the poet and critic Sir Herbert Read, his novels include *Game in Heaven with Tussy Marx*, *The Junkers*, and *A Married Man*. He has also written *Alive* and *The Train Robbers*. He lives in Yorkshire and France.

ROSS, ALAN   155

Poet, writer on travel and cricket, and editor of the *London Magazine*. His works include *The Forties: A Period Piece*, *The Onion Man, Cape Summer and the Australians in England*, and *The Taj Express: Poems 1967–1973*.

Index of Contributors

stories, and is an interesting television playwright. His latest novel is *Other People's Worlds*.

TUOHY, FRANK   204

Novelist and short-story writer, the fusion of atmospheric power and sharp characterization in whose work gives it a keen edge. He has written *The Animal Game*, *The Ice Saints*, *Live Bait*, *Fingers in the Door*, and a biographical study of W. B. Yeats.

WILLIAMS, RAYMOND   215

Born in Wales and now lives in Cambridge, where he is a Fellow of Jesus College and Professor of Drama. His works include *Culture and Society*, *The Long Revolution*, *Modern Tragedy*, and *The Country and the City*. The latter book is now a classic of its kind.